D1551759

A VENTURE IN HISTORY

*The Production, Publication, and Sale of
the Works of Hubert Howe Bancroft*

Hubert Howe Bancroft. Courtesy Bancroft Library, University of California.

A VENTURE IN HISTORY

*The Production, Publication, and Sale of
the* Works *of Hubert Howe Bancroft*

BY

HARRY CLARK

UNIVERSITY OF CALIFORNIA PRESS
BERKELEY · LOS ANGELES · LONDON
1973

John Dewey Library
Johnson State College
Johnson, Vermont

.978.007
C548v
54-6072

University of California Publications

LIBRARIANSHIP: 19

Approved for publication July 14, 1971

University of California Press
Berkeley and Los Angeles
California

University of California Press, Ltd.
London, England

ISBN: 0-520-09417-4
Library of Congress Catalog Card No.: 72-173900

© 1973 by the Regents of the University of California
Printed in the United States of America

For Margaret

CONTENTS

PREFACE

Between 1874 and 1890, Hubert Howe Bancroft, a San Francisco publisher and bookseller, produced, from the resources of his unparalleled collection of books and manuscripts on the West, his *Works*—a thirty-nine-volume social and historical study of the western portion of North America. The volumes (see pp. xii–xiii, below) form the most detailed account of the area as a whole that has ever been written and are still considered as fundamental reference tools today. They could not have been produced by a lone historian and would not have been produced if Bancroft had not been confident of selling them.

Bancroft's use of assistants in writing and his sanction of the sale of the *Works* by canvassing have embarrassed his apologists and delighted unfriendly critics, but both the hired writers and the book agents were necessary to secure completion of his history. The present study explores in detail the participation of both Bancroft and his associates in the production, publication, and sale of the *Works*, and attempts to estimate the success of their efforts.

These efforts began with the compilation of the first volumes before 1874 and continued to 1892, when the canvass was abandoned. Despite his delegation of writing and other matters, Bancroft was constantly involved (as his letters to William Nemos and others of his staff show) in research for the work, direction of its production, printing and publication, and assistance in its sale. In 1891, economic pressures caused him to publish the *Chronicles of the Builders of the Commonwealth*, a seven-volume vanity biography, which was presented as a sequel to the *Works*. Despite its shortcomings, the *Chronicles* was tied to the *Works* because of the manner of its introduction to subscribers, its production and its publication. The inevitable exposure of the biography hurt the history by association. The publication of the *Chronicles* forms a part of the story of the *Works* and must be considered in any account of the campaign for the larger set. Changes in the structure of the Bancroft corporations during the campaign are also considered, as they affected publication and returns. The study concludes with an appraisal of Bancroft's contribution to publishing and to history.

The primary source for details of Bancroft's life to 1890 is his autobiography, *Literary Industries*. Any factual material in this study not attributed to another source will be found here. *"Literary Industries" in a New Light* by Henry Oak, an exposé published by one of the writers of the *Works*, gives information on the portions of the histories written by hired writers, as do the letters and diary of Frances Fuller Victor and letters written by Bancroft to William Nemos. The originals of the letters to Nemos are deposited in the Kungl. Biblioteket of Stockholm, but a microfilm copy is in the Bancroft Library of the University of California.

The information presented in this study could not have been recovered without the assistance of many people. I am happy to acknowledge the helpfulness of Mr. Robert Becker and the staff of the Bancroft Library, who trusted me with some of their yet-to-be-cataloged wealth of materials. In other collections I was helped greatly by Dr. William N. Davis Jr., Historian of the California State Archives; Dr. Edwin Carpenter, Bibliographer at the Huntington Library; Mr. Alan R. Ottley, Curator of the California Room of the California State Library and Mr. Richard C Berner, formerly Curator of Manuscripts of the University of Washington Library. Correspondence elicited cooperation from many other librarians.

I should also like to express my gratitude to several people who read the manuscript: Dr. James D. Hart, Dr. Patrick Wilson, Mr. James Sisson, and Dr. Walton Bean, who also first aroused my interest in Bancroft. I owe a particular debt to Dr. Robert D. Harlan and Dr. Fredric Mosher for their care in reviewing the text and their many suggestions.

A NOTE ON STYLE

SHORT TITLES for various volumes of the *Works* are ordinarily used in the text, for example, *Central America* I for the *History of Central America*, volume I. In the same manner, the *History of the Pacific States* is frequently abbreviated to *History*.

Bancroft's collection is referred to as the Bancroft library until its sale to the University of California. The Bancroft Library is used to designate the institution within the University. Directly quoted material may show exceptions to this rule.

THE *WORKS* OF HUBERT HOWE BANCROFT

CHAPTER I

A CALIFORNIA BOOKMAN

FOR FORTY-SIX years, from the day he began work for his first employer in 1848, until he closed the doors of his great San Francisco
store for the last time in 1894, Hubert Howe Bancroft was a book
dealer. During that period he had also won renown as a historian, but,
proud as he was of this distinction, his business remained vitally important to him. He was crushed when his store was destroyed by fire
in 1886, and he closed a rebuilt store in 1894 only after a long and
bitter price war had made the business unprofitable.

Bancroft's ability to collect material for his history and to sustain
the expense of writing the inital volumes depended on the prosperity
of his business. The completion of the set depended on the skill with
which he marketed the first volumes. The daring, persistence, and
enterprise developed by the pursuit of business success was vital to
the organization and direction of his venture into historiography.
The virtues of persistence and enterprise, however, had been precepts
of his childhood.

Bancroft was born in Granville, Ohio, in 1832, where his parents,
Azariah Ashley Bancroft and Lucy Howe, brought him up in accordance with the standards of the community. It was a Puritan
town, the product of a group migration from Granville, Massachusetts, and the Puritan ethic was very much in power. Laziness was the

root of all evil, and work and thrift were given moral force.[1] Work and thrift, however, never provided Bancroft's parents with a comfortable living. In 1840, when Bancroft was eight years old, his father sold his house and farm in Granville and took the family to Missouri on a farming venture that failed. Within three years the family returned to Granville without a house and farm.[2] The experience may well have impressed the boy with the necessity for shrewdness in addition to industry.

In 1848, Bancroft went to Buffalo to work in a bookstore owned by his brother-in-law, George Derby. Derby, determined to show no partiality, nagged him unmercifully, and the sixteen-year-old boy was miserable. After six interminable months, he was discharged. Although Derby would not acknowledge Bancroft's ability in the shop, he thought well enough of the youth's efficiency and integrity to let him have a load of books on consignment for sale in Ohio. Bancroft did well and returned to the bookstore's employ in triumph. He spent the next two years of his life in riotous living, a strutting young gallant, experimenting with the temptations of the world and finding them irresistible. In later years, he was to deplore this period as a waste of precious time, but he acknowledged its purgative function, as the seamier diversions of pioneer California never attracted him.[3]

Bancroft kept his indulgences from his family, and his bouts of yielding to temptation and moping in remorse could not have interfered with his work, for Derby determined to send him to California with a consignment of books. Derby had sent three shipments of books to the Pacific Coast in 1851. Two were lost, but one yielded a profit of seventy-five percent. This high return and a letter from Bancroft's father, who had gone to the gold fields in 1850, fixed his determination to send a really large shipment to be sold by his own agents. Bancroft also was fired with enthusiasm by his father's letter and asked only that George Kenny, a bosom friend and fellow clerk,

---

[1] John Walton Caughey, *Hubert Howe Bancroft; Historian of the West* (Berkeley and Los Angeles: University of California Press, 1946), 7.

[2] Hubert Howe Bancroft, *Literary Industries, Works*, XXXIX (San Francisco: History Company, 1890), 77–78.

[3] Ibid., 110–116.

accompany him. Permission was readily given, and the pair left New York for Panama and California in February of 1852.[4]

The voyage was typically rigorous for the times. The United States Steamship Company operated the New York-Panama portion and overcrowded their vessels to the limits of navigability.[5] Steaming through the rough Atlantic to Havana was a miserable, sordid experience for Bancroft, who found most of his gold-seeking fellow-voyagers boorish or silly.[6]

Passengers changed ship at Havana, however, and the city enchanted the twenty-year-old youth. A day driving through orange groves and blossoming trees, and an evening watching dark-eyed girls, half-veiled in mantillas, strolling about a moon-drenched plaza, showed him a world as foreign to Ohio and New York as it was to the crowded ship. The filth of Colon disgusted him, but despite his distaste for that city and for the arduous trip by rail, boat, and mule-back through Panama to the Pacific, he was fascinated by all he saw.[7]

Bancroft found the trip pleasanter on the Pacific side, although a storm threatened to wrench the ship apart. He and Kenny arrived in San Francisco on April 1, 1852.

San Francisco was booming, changing rapidly from a town into a city. Swept by fires in 1850 and 1851, the city had risen again. Brick buildings and plank streets were now common, and new flat land suitable for business development was being created by leveling the sand hills and filling the shallow water of Yerba Buena cove.[8] Among its many commercial establishments, San Francisco counted twelve bookstores with stocks ranging from the fifty thousand volumes of standard authors, available from Cooke and Le Count, to the probably equivalent number of paperback thrillers sold by Charles P. Kimball, "The Noisy Carrier."[9]

[4] Ibid., 119–121.

[5] Hubert Howe Bancroft, *California Inter Pocula, Works* XXXV (San Francisco: History Company, 1888), 125–128.

[6] Ibid., 137–150.

[7] Ibid., 151–152, 156–189.

[8] Ibid., 261.

[9] Hugh Sanford Cheney Baker, "A History of the Book Trade in California," *California Historical Society Quarterly*, XXX (June, 1951), 107–109.

Although the number and prosperity of bookstores were of vital concern to the young men from Buffalo, they were more impressed with the frontier aspects of the city. The pair spent their evenings wandering in and out of gambling houses, gazing at the rough men and fancy women gathered around the tables.

After two days in port, Bancroft and Kenny took a steamboat for Sacramento. They found that city, although prosperous from trade with the mines, less hectic and challenging than San Francisco. After they had seen a little of the town, they consulted Barton, Reid and Grimm, a firm of commission merchants. The older men confirmed the wisdom of the youth's inclination to open shop in the inland city, and Bancroft wrote Derby to that effect.[10]

In 1852 there were eight bookstores in Sacramento, for from the beginning of the Gold Rush, as Derby had found out, books had sold well in California. Both Marysville and Stockton had bookstores, too. Letters and diaries of agents of the San Francisco book houses show that every mining camp had a bookshelf in its general store, and several towns in the Sierra foothills including Georgetown, Coloma, Sonora, and Downieville had small bookstores.[11] Nevertheless, Bancroft and Kenny thought there was room for one more.

While awaiting the arrival of the books, which would take eight or nine months by way of Cape Horn, the two young men went to the diggings to look for Bancroft's father and brother. The elder Bancroft was at the time a working shareholder in the Plymouth quartz mine near Long Bar, and Bancroft settled down for a time to help his father, hauling rock from mine to mill and gathering wood to burn and reduce the ore. Chafing under the hard physical labor of lifting rock and wood and of driving a team of mules, he hauled twice as many loads as was expected of him—enraged at the mules and at himself.

The mine was a failure, although the Bancrofts were reluctant to believe it. But after two months, when the hot weather came, they abandoned the mine—receiving pay for their labors in the form of worthless shares of stock. The older Bancroft returned to Granville

[10] Bancroft, *Literary Industries*, 123–124.
[11] Baker, *California Historical Society Quarterly*, XXX, 109–112.

after a brief visit to Rich Bar to see another of his sons, while the younger remained in Rich Bar for the summer, helping his brother manage the Empire, a canvas-covered structure of rough boards which served as a hotel.[12]

The Empire reputedly had been designed as a bordello, but the enterprise had failed, and Curtis Bancroft bought the building for a few hundred dollars.[13] Its most conspicuous feature was an elegantly fitted bar on the ground floor with a magnificent mirror. Bancroft must have found the establishment as curious, and its calico-covered walls as garish, as did Louise Smith Clappe, who described the hotel vividly to her sister[14]—but Bancroft was not in a position to share her detached amusement. She was a doctor's wife and one of four or five women in camp; Bancroft had no privileges of position or sex.

Although the flumes and rockers along the Feather River probably impressed the youth as much as they did Mrs. Clappe, Bancroft barely mentions Rich Bar in his writings. Many of the citizens were like the passengers who had disgusted him on the ship to Panama. The entire summer and fall must have been an ordeal to him. He wrote later: "Some woods send forth fragrance under the tool of the carver. Such was not my nature. I never took kindly to misfortune; prosperity fits me like a glove."[15]

Upon his return from Rich Bar to Sacramento in November 1852, Bancroft received news of Derby's death. Realizing that his hopes of opening a bookshop in Sacramento were gone, he was still obliged to remain in California until the consignment of books already shipped could reach him and be disposed of. The waiting period passed slowly, and Bancroft felt the humiliation of unsuccessfully seeking work in San Francisco. Kenny, who had spent the summer at Indian

---

[12] Bancroft, *Literary Industries*, 129–131.

[13] [Louise Amelia Knapp Smith Clappe], *The Shirley Letters from the California Mines, 1851-1852*, with introduction and notes by Carl I. Wheat (New York: Knopf, 1961), 27–28.

Mrs. Clappe repeated what she had been told about the origin of the Empire, as it was a hotel when she arrived, and Bancroft stated (*Literary Industries*, 125) that his brother "erected a building and put up a store" in Rich Bar.

[14] Clappe, 23–26.

[15] Bancroft, *Literary Industries*, 128.

Bar, also working for Curtis Bancroft, formed a partnership with William P. Cooke, late of Cooke and Le Count, and arranged to sell the books on consignment on their arrival. After showing a brotherly solicitude in the disposal of the book stock, Bancroft left San Francisco for Crescent City.

The latter city, a shabby trading post at the time, was expected to become the center for a new gold rush. Gold was being mined at Althouse and Jacksonville a short distance over the border in Oregon and was reported on the Smith River only twelve miles away. New finds were anticipated. Crescent City, the nearest port, would boom if a big strike came.[16]

Bancroft took along a case of books procured on credit and went to work as a bookkeeper in a general store for fifty dollars a month with the privilege of placing his books on the shelf and selling them. He spent little and made large profits, which he loaned to the firm. He was given salary increases as his duties grew, so that, after eighteen months, he was receiving $250 monthly (some of it in interest). After twenty-four months, the business failed. Bancroft's ventures netted him a few thousand dollars in two and a half years, and with this he built a store, left it in the hands of an agent, and returned to New York.[17]

Despite the comforts of the East, Auburn and Buffalo seemed very tame to Bancroft after California, for, as he wrote later: "the western coast with all its rough hardships and impetuous faults so fascinating, had fastened itself too strongly upon me to be shaken off." The dreary voyage, the rough companions, were as nothing compared to the challenge of the West where "all was new, all was to be done."[18]

In 1856 Bancroft believed he was strong enough to succeed in business in San Francisco, and he was eager to try. He rejected the soft life of the East, exclaiming: "I must be something of myself, and do

---

[16] Ibid., 136–137.

[17] Ibid., 137–139. Bancroft gave his returns as "six or eight thousand dollars," but W. C. Ferril, "A Basis for Western Literature," *Commonwealth*, Denver, I (1889), 79, gave the amount as three or four thousand dollars. The article is a report of an interview, and the sum was given as a direct quotation from Bancroft.

[18] Bancroft, *Literary Industries*, 143–144.

something by myself: it is the Me and not money that cries for activity and development."[19]

The capital to begin this development was offered to him by his sister, Celia, George Derby's widow, who, when she learned of his determination to return to San Francisco, asked him to use the money realized from the sale of Derby's shipment of books in California. Mrs. Derby rejected a partnership in Bancroft's proposed enterprise and accepted instead a note made payable in five or six years bearing 1 percent per month interest.

Bancroft determined to carry out Derby's own plans with his money and, after contracting for stock, sailed again for San Francisco. On his arrival he looked up his old friend Kenny, whose firm had failed. Bancroft took Kenny into partnership and began business as H. H. Bancroft and Company in a rented room on Montgomery and Merchant streets in December 1856.

The next twelve years saw the business grow steadily from its modest beginnings. Bancroft determined to use credit to obtain consignments of goods, and on his first trip to the East on the firm's behalf obtained goods to the amount of sixty or seventy thousand dollars. In 1857, he entered publishing with *Reports of Cases Determined in the District Courts of California* by Henry J. Labatt, v. 1, no. 1.[20] From 1860 law was to be the backbone of his publishing business. Twenty-five titles, nearly one-third of Bancroft's total list of seventy-nine titles published between 1860 and 1870 are in law,[21] and law books were his only dependable sellers.[22]

However, a favorable trading situation did as much or more for the firm's prosperity than its active publishing program. Because of the inflation of currency which occurred during the Civil War, he was able to obtain goods in the East with paper money, and sell them

[19] Ibid., 144.

[20] Unpublished bibliography, which I gathered between January and May 1965. University of California Law Library has one copy of *Reports* I:I; imprint is on paper cover, not on title page.

[21] Ibid.

[22] "I almost always lost money on whatever I would publish there [San Francisco] because of the light demand, except for law books, which were profitable." Bancroft quoted by Ferril in *Commonwealth*, I, 76.

in California for gold. Years later Albert Bancroft, Hubert's brother, explained how this benefited the firm. A purchase of an item costing $1.00 in currency in New York could be sold for $2.00 gold in San Francisco. With the $2.00 in gold the company bought New York exchange currency at 250 percent and received $5.00 for what had originally cost $1.00. Celia Derby's loan was repaid in gold, and the business continued to expand.[23] In 1868, the Montgomery Street quarters had become so crowded that a move was necessary, so Bancroft bought property on Market Street, near Third, and began to build in 1869.

In April 1870 the new building was completed. Behind the imposing iron front, construction was entirely of wood and brick. There were five floors, measuring 75×170 feet, and a full basement, which contained a steam engine to provide power for printing presses and other machinery, and an artesian well.[24]

Space in four floors of the building was divided to accommodate nine departments. The nature of these departments shows the directions in which Bancroft had moved since beginning his career in San Francisco. Six dealt directly with customers and were on the first floor. These included the wholesale and retail book and stationery departments, the music department (featuring pianos and sheet music), the bank and official department (selling blank books, ledgers, and other business forms), the law department, and the education department. The subscription book department was on the second floor, the printing department occupied the entire third floor, and a bindery and blank book factory took up all of the fourth floor.[25]

Four of the departments—music, education, printing, and binding —were headed by young Bancrofts, nephews of the proprietor. Bancroft's old friend Kenny supervised the bank and official department. F. P. Stone, who had managed the sale of law books for the Montgomery Street establishment, headed the law department.[26] Bancroft

[23] Albert Little Bancroft, "Statement," one-page typewritten manuscript, Society of California Pioneers Library, San Francisco.

[24] "A Cosmopolitan Publishing House; History of the Establishment of A. L. Bancroft and Co., San Francisco, Cal.," *Paper World*, XII (March, 1881), 2–3.

[25] Ibid., 3–5.   [26] Ibid.

chose men as department heads whom he believed bound to him by ties of blood or long loyalty, and he gave them almost complete responsibility and autonomy.

The printing division was one of the most successful departments in the firm. The press had been an independent establishment, as was the bindery. Bancroft purchased them and placed them under the supervision of W. B. Bancroft, a nephew, who managed them capably and profitably. Aside from letterpress work, the printing shop did a lively business in lithography, turning out greeting cards, illustrations, and labels. In one season, over twenty million labels were turned out for Pacific Coast salmon canneries.[27] The profits helped the entire firm to remain solvent during periods of economic depression.

The pressroom and bindery naturally took over the preparation of Bancroft's own publications. Books published by Bancroft were sold in all first-floor departments except the music department, and a subdivision of the educational department sold Bancroft's maps.[28] Although the law books comprised the most important publications at the time, the firm also issued and promoted a series of readers and spellers. Bancroft's list of general publications included religion, fiction, biography, and many works of local interest.

One of the books in the last category was *Bancroft's Pacific States Almanac*, first issued in 1862. The work is reputed to have given Bancroft the impulse to begin his collection of books on the West. In 1859 or 1862 (accounts differ), either Bancroft or William H. Knight, a map-maker in his employ, had gathered all the books on California and the West in Bancroft's stock on shelves near Knight's desk to aid him in writing the *Almanac*. According to Knight's account, which gives the later date, Bancroft had been in the East when the collection was made, and on his return requested Knight to "visit all the other bookstores and stands in the city and purchase a copy of every book and pamphlet relating to this territory that is not already on your shelves."[29] Whether Bancroft or Knight made

[27] Ibid., 5. [28] Ibid., 4–5.
[29] Bertha Knight Power, *William Henry Knight, California Pioneer* ([n.p.] 1932), 37, also Los Angeles *Times*, March 10, 1918. For Bancroft's account see *Literary Industries*, 175–197.

the original collection, Bancroft was soon gathering books omni-
vorously from San Francisco and from cities he visited on his eastern
trips. He enlarged his field of collection from California to the western half of America, and he collected everything—books, pamphlets,
or manuscripts—that he could find.

Although he had no defined purpose in making the collection, he
could not permit himself to become a bibliomaniac. His conscience
rebelled at the idea of collecting books as one would teacups, simply
because of their rarity, and he was determined to find an objective
that would make his activity dignified and noble. Until he could call
his collection complete, however, this rationale could wait.

In 1862, with a thousand volumes, he felt his work was almost
done, but a visit to the bookstores of Paris and London opened his
eyes. Bancroft returned to those cities and others in 1866–1867 with
his wife Emily, whom he had wed almost a decade earlier. Between
sightseeing excursions and more general shopping, he visited the
bookstores in Spain, Italy, France, and Switzerland. Before leaving
London, the collector engaged Joseph Whitaker, publisher of the
Bookseller, to act as his agent after his return to the United States.[30]

In January 1869 Bancroft telegraphed five thousand dollars earnest
money to Whitaker so that the latter might purchase books at the
Leipzig auction from the Andrade collection. José María Andrade
had, during forty years, collected seven thousand items concerning
Mexico or printed in that country from 1543. Andrade had agreed
to sell the collection to Maximilian for the foundation of a *Biblioteca
Imperial de Mejico*, but after the emperor's fall, the collector fled
Mexico, taking the books with him. The collection contained, besides six volumes printed in Mexico between 1543 and 1547, unique
books and documents on the history of the Spanish domination of
Mexico from the time of Cortez to the War of Independence.[31]
Whitaker secured nearly half the books on sale, and his choices delighted Bancroft, as they increased his collection "with some three
thousand of the rarest and most valuable volumes extant."[32]

Bancroft continued to buy at auctions of private libraries in the

---

[30] Bancroft, *Literary Industries*, 178–185.
[31] Ibid., 185–189.   [32] Ibid., 190.

United States and in Europe. By 1869 there were sixteen thousand volumes to be placed on the fifth floor of the new Market Street building. This floor was to be a literary workshop, completely divorced from the business, where Bancroft's treasured library could be put to use. Bancroft lined the walls with books, placed tables in the center of the floor, and engaged a librarian to catalog the works which he had acquired. He knew that his collection was not complete (he continued to purchase books at notable sales until 1880), but he could no longer neglect the problem of what to do with it. He wanted to create some sort of literary monument out of his raw material.[33]

Because of these aspirations, Bancroft placed the firm in his younger brother's name, calling it A. L. Bancroft and Company. Albert Little Bancroft, the titular head of the new firm, had come with his brother to California in 1859, in a party which included Hubert Bancroft's bride Emily, and his sister Mary Melissa. In 1860 the elder Bancroft had placed his brother at the head of a short-lived business in a building on Clay Street to sell stationery and blank books. Albert was not quite nineteen and lived with Hubert and Emily. With the dissolution of the stationery business, Albert had entered the firm of H. H. Bancroft and Company. Although he had married, the two families continued to share the same residence until Emily Bancroft's death in 1869, and Albert and his wife lived with Hubert until 1871.[34] The dominance of the older brother in business and personal affairs was never challenged until, years later, a quarrel severed their relations.

The recession which followed the opening of the transcontinental railway in 1869 kept Hubert Bancroft active in the management of A. L. Bancroft and Company, as his wholesale trade suffered from eastern competition. His interest, however, was no longer exclusively in business, and he continued to pursue plans to use his huge library.

[33] Ibid., 197, 219–223.
[34] Henry Raup Wagner, "Albert Little Bancroft, His Diaries, Account Books, and Card String of Events," *California Historical Society Quarterly*, XXIX (June, 1950,) 99.

Chapter II

THE PREPARATION OF A HISTORY

Bancroft did not hit at once upon the idea of publishing a history, but thought of compiling a *Pacific Encyclopedia*, which would feature contributions by many writers on "physical geography, geology, botany, ethnology, history, biography, and so on through the whole range of knowledge."[1] Several important western figures agreed to contribute articles at Bancroft's request. The history and biography in the encyclopedia were to be enriched by information from living men, and Bancroft sent letters to California pioneers soliciting material on the early settlement of the state.

Many pioneers responded enthusiastically. John Rose of Smartsville sent in the names of all the pioneers that he could remember, and offered the names of three other pioneers as sources of further information.[2] Albert G. Toomes wrote Bancroft from Tehama on June 21, 1872:

> I . . . refer you to a letter of mine written some years ago giving the names of most of the Early Settlers of this Coast. This you will find in the Cali-

[1] Bancroft, *Literary Industries*, 224.
[2] Rose to Bancroft, April 2 and July 27, 1872 [History Company Records]. History Company Records is the title provisionally assigned to a large collection of uncataloged manuscripts concerning Bancroft and his publications in the Bancroft Library. I have used brackets in citing this source to indicate that the title is unofficial at time of writing.

fornia Scrap Book on pages 180, 181, 182, 183 and 184 this is the most correct that has bin published but still it is not correct Wm. Moore should be Wm. Moon who still lives in this County and there is many others which I think you can git from some of the old pioneers.[3] [*sic*]

Other letters which have been preserved offer to send photographs for what most of the pioneers seem to have felt would be a collection of biographies.

Despite the responses of the pioneers and many would-be contributors, Bancroft lost interest in the projected encyclopedia because he was aware that contributors expected to be given access to his collection, which would have to be put in shape for their use. He, himself, had literary aspirations and was alternately writing enthusiastically and discarding the disappointing results. His health failed, and, moody and irritable, he returned to New York to visit his sister and friends, leaving the business under Albert's care and the library under the supervision of Henry Oak, a young man who had entered the Bancroft offices to edit a religious paper and, on its demise, remained as cataloger and librarian of Bancroft's collection. During Bancroft's visit in the East a woman friend, perhaps provoked by his moodiness, challenged him, telling him that his next ten years could be the most productive of his life and asking him what he intended doing with them. The subject was very much in Bancroft's thoughts, and as he had been well aware for some time of the value of his collection to a historian, he resolved to become that historian: "History-writing I conceived to be the highest of human occupatons, and this should be my choice, were my ability equal to my ambition."[4]

In preparation for the *Pacific Encyclopedia*, Oak had begun indexing information in many of the works after his initial task of preparing an author-title card file of the collection, and had also, with Bancroft's approval, cut up duplicate copies of works to separate the subjects of which they treated. Bancroft had long realized the necessity for an index and key to the material in the thousands of books he had acquired, but many experiments were required to find the most efficient methods to make this instrument. Copying by a crew of

[3] Toomes to Bancroft, June 21, 1872 [History Company Records].
[4] Bancroft, *Literary Industries*, 229.

men was tried and abandoned as time consuming and inaccurate. A detailed subject index was attempted, but was not successful, according to Bancroft, until a standardized list of subject headings was devised. Bancroft's description of the index on cards which evolved makes it appear very much like an analytic library subject catalog of today.

An annotated subject index to the collection was, of course, essential to the project to which Bancroft now set himself, the writing of a history of western America. He stated:

> My object seemed to be the pride and satisfaction it would afford me to improve somewhat the records of my race, save something of a nation's history which but for me would drop into oblivion . . . to originate and perfect a system by which means alone the history could be gathered and written; . . . and accomplish in one generation . . . what might never have been accomplished at all. Mine was a great work that could be accomplished by a small man.[5]

The system that Bancroft originated and sought to perfect in order to gather materials for his history involved the extensive use of assistants. They, of course, cataloged the library, but Bancroft used them in all stages of the work. Fifteen or twenty were employed at making references and "taking out material," together with the men indexing newspapers, "epitomizing" archives, and copying manuscripts. At times, there were as many as fifty men engaged in library detail.

Bancroft proposed to write the history of the "Pacific States," his own term for all of North America from the Pacific eastward to the states lying on the Continental Divide, and from Panama northward to Alaska. The inclusion of Central America and Mexico permitted him to retell the story of the conquistadores, which appealed to him strongly. Their inclusion was logical, however, as much of the western United States had formerly belonged to Mexico. The territory was well chosen for sales also, as several of his American patrons had served in the Mexican War, and many had come west as he did via Panama. The curiosity of the Americans about the lands they had seen would incline them to read a history of those countries.

[5] Ibid., 286.

Bancroft was well aware that in order to form the basis of a history his collection should be enriched and extended by manuscript records, which he could not hope to purchase in conventional sales, and by information from participants in the events which he planned to narrate. The response of California pioneers to the *Pacific Encyclopedia* had shown their interest in giving such information. Through personal visits with pioneers, members of distinguished Mexican families, and public officials, Bancroft continued to search for material.

In 1874 he went with his daughter, Kate, and Henry Oak to visit San Diego, Los Angeles, and other parts of southern California. During his wedding trip with his second bride, Matilda Griffing Bancroft, in the summer of 1876, he called on John Sutter in Lititz, Pennsylvania. Bancroft tarried, taking dictation from Sutter for five days, while his new wife sat nearby. He traveled through the Pacific Northwest in 1878, to Mexico City in 1883, to Utah and Colorado in 1884, and made many shorter trips in order to solicit manuscripts or record dictated memoirs.

One of the fruits of his travels was the acquisition of the collection of Judge Benjamin Hayes. Hayes, a Roman Catholic resident of San Diego, had been given authority to examine Church records and had copies of records made by Father Serra and his successor, as well as early pueblo archives. The judge was very interested in Bancroft's work and, after a little persuasion, offered his papers to the library. In March of 1875 Bancroft thanked him in a letter which shows justifiable pride in his own progress:

My dear Judge
  What you have written will be intensely interesting to me and of great value to the state. There is no fear of their [*sic*] being too much of it. I have had a can made to stand in the middle of the room to hold your collection, Gen. Vallejo's and others of that kind—that is, California History. Gen. Vallejo has just about finished a Hist. of Cal. for me. Gov. Alvarado also and Castro is writing. Now it just takes yours to make the thing complete . . . . Your Coll. will be quoted by me in subsequent work thousands of times and always under the name of "Hayes Coll."[6]

[6] Bancroft to Hayes, March 16, 1875. California State Library, Sacramento, California.

To complete his picture of the West, Bancroft sought economic and social information as well as historical and political data. After writing his regrets to Edward Huggins on "not seeing you during my later visit to the north," Bancroft promised to make good use of anything Huggins might write for him concerning the Hudson Bay Company forts, "the founding of the towns, the settlement of any part of the country, the opening of any mines; the coal, agricultural, grazing, saw-mill, or any other interest; Indian battles. . . ." Characteristically, Bancroft cautioned Huggins against being afraid to write anything down, no matter how trifling it might seem, and told him that the more he wrote the better Bancroft would like it. Bancroft concluded: "It is a very important work I am engaged in, and I am very sure when it is done you will not regret having a hand in it."[7]

Some of Bancroft's correspondents did come to regret having a hand in it because the historian was less scrupulous about returning material than gathering it. In two undated letters to Clarence Booth Bagley, a Washington (State) printer and publisher, Bancroft requested information, assuring him that this information would make separate treatment for Washington, Idaho, and Montana possible, where inclusion in the Oregon volumes had been originally intended. In October of 1882, Bancroft wrote to say that Bagley's papers had been very useful and that he would like to retain them a little longer. He offered Bagley a "regular receipt for them, if you will send me down a list of just exactly what I received from you," and reiterated his gratitude while requesting more later material on Washington for his history. At the close he wrote: "All material you will kindly loan me will be as safe as it is possible for anything to be in this world." Further correspondence between Bagley and Bancroft and his commercial assistants, F. P. Stone and Nathan Stone, extends to January of 1895 and indicates that Bagley recovered only a part of the material he had submitted, as he could not or would not submit a detailed list of titles and dates. The rest remained "as safe as it is possible" in the Bancroft collection.[8]

[7] Bancroft to Huggins, July 9, 1878. Henry E. Huntington Library, San Marino, California.

[8] All correspondence from *C. B. Bagley Collection*, University of Washington, Seattle, Washington.

Bancroft used some of his assistants to help in the work of gathering information, and one of them gained material for the history that Bancroft probably could not have obtained through anyone else. The historian lacked the qualities of gentility to recommend him to the Mexican-Californians, but Enrique Cerruti, an Italian soldier of fortune, had them in abundance. A flamboyant and slightly foolish-appearing figure to American eyes, Cerruti appealed to the old Californians, and this appeal won for Bancroft and his enterprise the support, documents, and dictations of General Mariano Vallejo, Governor Juan B. Alvarado, and Manuel Castro. The courtly Italian with a fluent command of Spanish became fast friends with Vallejo, who enthusiastically helped Bancroft in his search for California records for two and a half years.

Thomas Savage, a master of the Spanish language, did important service with documents in that tongue. Before he came to the library in 1873, Savage had been for twenty-one years in the American consulate in Havana and had worked in Central America. He became Bancroft's main authority on Spanish-American affairs and took many dictations for him from Spanish-speaking Californians in Salinas, San José, Los Angeles, San Diego, and other cities. He also copied mission archives in San Juan Capistrano, San Gabriel, and Santa Cruz. In 1876–1877, he directed a crew of Bancroft employees in abstracting the archives of California collected in the Surveyor General's office in San Francisco. Gathered from all over the state in 1851, the archives dated from the period of the founding of the missions, and were, when Savage began, a "jumble." After ten months and the expenditure of $10,000, Savage and his crew had epitomized them in rational order in sixty-three volumes. Simple copying of the documents, he estimated, would have cost $40,000.[9]

Edward F. Murray was engaged by Bancroft to copy the archives of the Santa Barbara mission in June of 1876. He worked for over a year, adding twelve manuscripts volumes of Santa Barbara records, and one volume each from Santa Buenaventura, Santa Inés, and La Purísima missions to the library collections.

[9] Thomas Savage, "Report of Labor on Archives and Processing Material for History of California" (handwritten), 4–5. Bancroft Library.

In July 1878 Bancroft sent Ivan Petroff to Alaska. A Russian-born veteran of the Union Army, Petroff had spent the five years immediately following the Civil War near Fort Sitka. From there he had come to San Francisco and had entered Bancroft's employ in 1870. During his journey to Alaska as a Bancroft employee, Petroff examined archives at Fort Sitka, Kodiak, and Unalaska, and took many dictations. After his return to San Francisco, he was sent to Washington to examine archives of the Russian-American Fur Company housed in the State Department.

Bancroft acknowledged the services of all these assistants in his autobiography, *Literary Industries*.[10] He also paid tribute to his second wife, who served as assistant when they traveled together.[11] Two sentences in *Literary Industries*, at the close of a brief biography of Frances Fuller Victor, the only woman among the assistants, allege that Mrs. Victor was cooperating enthusiastically in assembling materials with which she was already familiar.[12] Mrs. Victor was indeed gathering data, but not enthusiastically. She worked at the library because she had to support herself, and she was unhappy with the slight acknowledgment she anticipated. In a letter to Elwood Evans, a local historian of Olympia, Washington, she expressed herself:

> I find time to write letters that concern my work—I write a good many to find out things, and put a good deal of material into the history which would not otherwise be there: in short, work just as conscientiously as if I were doing it for my own glory, and put into Mr. B's hands and under his name all the results of my long preparation for this particular work. . . .[13]

Except for the information solicited by Mrs. Victor for her own writing, all manuscripts collected by Bancroft and his assistants were indexed and noted. Like the material already in the library, the documents were then ready for the next step, the writing of the *Works*. The primary task of Bancroft's ablest assistants was not research but

[10] On Cerruti, *Literary Industries*, 365–444, on Savage, ibid., 523–529, on Murray, ibid., 512–522, on Petroff, ibid., 272, 551–561.

[11] Ibid., 458–459, 535–536, 761.

[12] Ibid., 261.

[13] Victor to Evans, January 7, 1880, in Evans, "Correspondence and Papers," Western Americana Collection, Yale University Library.

writing. Oak, Mrs. Victor, William Nemos, and others wrote nearly twenty-nine of the thirty-nine volumes which Bancroft published under his own name.

Bancroft had not anticipated allowing pages of the *Works* to go from the tables of the assistants to the printing shop with only superficial attempts at rewriting. *Literary Industries* contains an extended account of his "literary workshop" as it had been intended to function. Assistants, assigned duties in proportion to ther skills, occupied themselves with consulting authorities, note-taking, consolidating and compressing material, and citing and ranking references. Their reports were supposed to give Bancroft "a sort of bird's-eye view of all the evidence" on the topics for his history, as he followed his own plan for writing, and enable him to avoid "the drudgery and loss of time in thoroughly studying any but the best authorities."[14]

In reality the method followed in writing the *Works* was less elaborate than the one described in *Literary Industries*. In an exposé of Bancroft's methods, Oak admitted that "at first we had some such preliminary system in view," but then claimed that the immensity of the work, and the necessity of publishing part of it before the whole was completed, compelled the abandonment of the idea.[15]

The immensity of the work and the pressure to publish, however, could not have seemed compelling factors in surrendering authorship of the *Native Races of the Pacific States*. Bancroft is credited with only 270 pages of the five-volume work.[16] His intense distaste for the subject and his marked impatience with drudgery were probably responsible for his relinquishing the writing. Bancroft originally intended to begin his history with the Spanish conquests of Central America and Mexico, and he actually began to write a volume on the conquest of Darien when the necessity of writing about the aborigines, who, he felt, were present"wherever I touched the conti-

[14] Bancroft, *Literary Industries*, 565–568.
[15] Henry Lebbeus Oak, *"Literary Industries" in a New Light; a Statement on the Authorship of Bancroft's Native Races and History of the Pacific States* (San Francisco: Bacon Printing Co., 1893), 32.
[16] Henry Lebbeus Oak and William Nemos, "Estimate of the Authorship of the *Native Races* and *History of the Pacific States*" (handwritten). In Henry L. Oak, "Correspondence and Papers." Bancroft Library.

nent with my Spaniards,"[17] led to the conception of the five-volume anthropological-historical study. After planning the structure of the *Native Races* and writing the chapter on the "Hyperboreans" (Eskimos) which begins the first volume, Bancroft did not trouble to rewrite any other part of the work in such a manner as to make it his own. Instead, according to Oak, a system quickly developed in which the notes were given directly to the most talented writers among the assistants, who made their own researches in their own way, reached their own conclusions, expressed them in their own language and sent them to the printer without anything but a superficial and hasty revision.[18]

In *Literary Industries*, Bancroft stressed the demands of business on him which interfered with his writing at this time, and mentioned that: "three dry years and five years of hard times followed the opening of the railway."[19] Bancroft's business was threatened by eastern competition after 1869, and he did not surrender control.

His travels also cut into time he might have used for writing. In addition to western journeys for research and business, Bancroft crossed the country several times to visit relatives in the East or to purchase stock for the bookstore.

Bancroft's absences from the workshop, whether merely downstairs or out of town, tended to make the pattern which began with the *Native Races* a permanent one. As the amount of text produced by the workshop grew, Bancroft gave up his aspirations of rewriting it and became more concerned with turning out an attractive, acceptable product at a reasonable cost. Most of his efforts on the *Works*, therefore, were spent as editor and publisher. His editorial functions included planning the contents of each volume and writing the prefaces. Bancroft, of course, also determined larger matters such as the length of the set (thirty-nine volumes), the number of volumes to be used in relating the history of each region or political subdivision of the "Pacific States," and the order in which the history would appear.

He resolved to begin the *History of the Pacific States* with Central

---

[17] Bancroft, *Literary Industries*, 295.
[18] Oak, *"Literary Industries" in a New Light*, 32.
[19] Bancroft, *Literary Industries*, 165.

America, despite the fact that materials were at hand to begin, as Oak wished, with California. Although no work had been done on the Spanish American countries beyond the completion of *Central America* I, it was published first, so that for succeeding volumes, "all must be taken from the sources and written just behind the printer."[20] Despite its practical inconveniences, Bancroft's plan to begin the *History* with the conquistadores is more logical and appealing than Oak's and Bancroft was intensely interested in obtaining a favorable reception for the set.

In order to win approval for his work, Bancroft sometimes called for editorial assistance from outsiders. Despite Oak's statement that the assistants reached their own conclusions, Bancroft did modify some of those conclusons in the case of *Central America* I at the behest of a "committee from the churches." The result was "a multitude of changes affecting nearly every page, so that it might have been as cheap to set up the type anew as change the plates."[21] Oak, the author of the words just quoted, admitted, however, that the toning down was probably an improvement.

Before beginning the *History of Utah*, Bancroft deftly handled another religious problem by engaging in a brief but earnest correspondence with the elders of the Church of Jesus Christ of Latter Day Saints, and securing the cooperation of one of their number, Franklin Dewey Richardson, to help him and assistant Alfred Bates in dealing with Mormonism in the history.[22] After the death of his first wife, Bancroft had no strong religious feelings, and consequently, no interest in either advocacy or polemic. If an unnecessary or exaggerated phrase could offend someone, it was deleted; if there were conflicting viewpoints, both were presented. Thus, in the *History of Utah*, while the text is written in terms sympathetic to the Mormons, some of the footnotes carry arguments against Smith's "revelations," accounts of misconduct and provocation by Mormons, and similar unfavorable material.

[20] Oak, *"Literary Industries" in a New Light*, 32.
[21] Ibid., 36.
[22] Bancroft, *Literary Industries*, 638–639. The phrase: "and his assistant, Alfred Bates," does not appear in this source; Bates' share in *Utah* has been acknowledged in various writings by Oak, Nemos, and Mrs. Victor.

The *History of Utah* did not go through the workshop as smoothly as Bancroft would have liked, and he wrote William Nemos about it from Denver in 1884.

> Keep all the men if you think best, only make them work. Mrs. Bancroft and I are doing twice as much work on Utah after it leaves their hands as ever Bates and Newkirk did. True, we have found some additional information, but they did not get in half the information they had.[23]

In this, as in most of his letters to Nemos, who succeeded Oak as librarian, Bancroft appears clearly the editor and publisher, and only incidentally the author.

Other letters to Nemos show Bancroft's concern over expenses. He complained frequently about the slowness of the work and attempted to make it move faster. "I don't exactly know why I don't get galleys faster," he commented in a letter accompanying the manuscript for *Central America* III, which Bancroft was returning so that Edward Newkirk, another assistant, could make the maps and forward it to the printer; in another letter: "let Bates finish Alaska and drive him forward on it as fast as possible . . . Alaska has cost 3 times what it ought to and so has Oregon."[24] On another occasion, Bancroft quashed a suggestion by Nemos for increasing the staff.

> I do not think it will be wise to put any more men writing history, unless it would hasten matters, and I don't believe it would, and I think the work would not be as good. I would much rather let some of the men go and so reduce expenses, as fast as you can spare them for these are hard times for money.[25]

A year later some of the tension had eased, and Bancroft wrote: "I

---

[23] Bancroft to Nemos, November 26, 1884. Copy on microfilm in Bancroft Library from Kungl. Biblioteket, Stockholm. The letters are numbered, either by Nemos or by the Kungl. Biblioteket, and references to them will give this number after the date, as they appear in numerical order on the microfilm. This letter is no. 21.

[24] Quotations from two letters, Bancroft to Nemos: (month and day omitted) 1885, no. 26, and November 29, 1883, no. 30.

[25] Bancroft to Nemos, November 7, 1884, no. 3.

want the Cal. vols. to be done about as well as they can without so very much regard to time on them."[26]

Bancroft experienced this conflict between the desire for excellence and the need for money throughout the writing and publishing of the *Works*. It expressed itself outwardly in moodiness and impatience. He could never understand why the assistants had difficulty in writing, as he came to look on his own writing as a blessed escape from business cares. He took the notes of researchers on those portions of the history that interested him and wrote rapidly (therefore economically) and, he believed, well. He was interested in the romantic figures of the past—conquistadores, explorers, and fur traders; his more colorful contemporaries—the Mexican-Californians, the gold-seekers, the San Francisco vigilantes, and the Mormons; and himself—Hubert Howe Bancroft, the businessman who became a historian. He wrote chapters and entire books on all of these subjects to the extent of ten volumes of the *Works*; the remainder of the writing he delegated to others.[27]

[26] Bancroft to Nemos, November, 1885, no. 15.

[27] Bancroft is generally acknowledged to have written the following portions of the *Works*: one-third of one volume in the *Native Races*; four and one-quarter volumes in the *History of the Pacific States*, principally in *Central America* I, *Mexico* I, *Northwest Coast* I, *British Columbia*, and *Utah*; *California Pastoral* (with some assistance from Thomas Savage); *California Inter Pocula* (except for 115 pages on the Modoc War by Mrs. Victor); *Popular Tribunals* I and II; *Essays and Miscellany*; and *Literary Industries* (with chapters on the library and assistants by William Nemos). *See* Oak and Nemos, "Estimate . . ." and William Alfred Morris, "The Origin and Authorship of the Bancroft Pacific States Publications; a History of a History," *Oregon Historical Quarterly*, IV (December, 1903), 355–356.

CHAPTER III

LITERARY ASSISTANTS

THE LITERARY assistants were under continuous pressure to produce text. For ten hours a day, six days a week, they consulted their sources and wrote. If Bancroft thought their work slow, he told them so. As he compared their labors over unfamiliar documents with his own hasty composition on his personal enthusiasms, he was frequently critical.

The resentment aroused by Bancroft's criticisms and the realization that they were to get no public acknowledgement for their work led the assistants to record and report their shares in the *Works*. What was meant to be the most private part of the Bancroft enterprise has become the most fully documented. Henry Oak, William Nemos, and Frances Fuller Victor, the assistants responsible for most of the *Works*, have all made public statements or left memoranda deposited in libraries recording their share in the history.

Henry Oak, according to his own statement, wrote about ten volumes of the *Works*, including the complete texts of *Native Races* IV, *North Mexican States* I, *Arizona* and *New Mexico*, and *California* I–V. His work also appears in *Native Races* I, II, V, *Central America* I, *California* VI, and *Northwest Coast* I, II.[1] Oak, unlike most of the assistants, wrote long consecutive sections of the history,

[1] Oak and Nemos, "Estimate...," also Oak, "*Literary Industries*" *in a New Light*, 42.

24

a task to which he devoted all of his time from 1880, the year William Nemos took his place as director of the library and its workers. It was a transfer agreeable to both, as Oak was delighted to be relieved of administrative responsibility and suffered no loss of salary or prestige. Nemos was given no authority over his predecessor, and Oak subsequently regarded the years 1880 to 1887 during which he did nothing but write his assigned volumes from the unequaled resources of the library as the happiest period of his life.[2]

William Nemos, Oak's successor as librarian and collaborator with him on the estimate of authorship compiled in 1886, said in a notarized statement in 1888:

> The only person not subordinated to me was the first holder of the Librarianship.... His control after 1880 was limited to the books; the staff of workers, including the assistant librarians, being subject to me. Lacking skill as a writer, only inferior sections could be entrusted to him, the leading parts of his own field being written by myself. His quickness of eye made him one of our most valued proofreaders.[3]

This disparaging comment is in strong contrast with the estimate made with Oak's collaboration only two years before, and Nemos made it after Oak had retired. Because of Oak's painful honesty about his own weaknesses in his autobiographical note,[4] and Nemos' efforts to enhance his own position,[5] Oak's version carries more conviction.

Certainly Bancroft would never pay the salary which Oak claimed to have received during the greater part of his employment, $200 per month plus room rent,[6] to any assistant who was doing the sort of

[2] Henry Lebbeus Oak, "Autobiography...," one page extract from his *Oak, Oaks, Oakes, Family Register of Nathaniel Oak* (Los Angeles: Out West Co., [1898]).

[3] William Nemos, "Besvuren Angift af den förnämsta skrifvars & redaktn of Bancroft's History of the Pacific States" (handwritten in English and Swedish), San Francisco, July 31, 1888. Copy on microfilm in Bancroft Library from Kungl. Biblioteket, Stockholm. 4 pp. To be noted below as Nemos, [Notarized statement].

[4] Oak, "Autobiography...."

[5] Erik Gren, "Herbert [*sic*] Howe Bancroft and Wilhelm Roos, Alias William Nemos," *Lychnos* (1950–1951), 49.

[6] Oak, *"Literary Industries" in a New Light*, 63.

work attributed to Oak by Nemos. Most of the assistants received from $20 to $23.10 for a sixty hour week, and though Nemos received more, his vagueness on the subject makes a comparison difficult. Nemos received "a salary double that of any other person on the staff. Only one other member ever enjoyed more than the half rate (i.e., half of my rate) assigned as the highest pay for the staff in general."[7] That member, of course, was Oak. Although Nemos was unfair to his predecessor, Oak must have been difficult, especially as his health began to fail. His self-portrait is one of an acknowledged failure, friendless, poor, sick, despondent, "but surprisingly free from morbid despair" as a result of "a sort of philosophic carelessness respecting most matters great and small."[8] He was a joyless man, and his negativism was completely alien to Bancroft and Nemos.

Oak retired in 1887 because of ill health, having remained silent up to that time as to his share in the writing of the *Works*. When *Literary Industries* was published in 1890 with Bancroft's statement: "To more experienced and able assistants were given the study and reduction of certain minor sections of the history, which I employed in my writing with more or less condensation and change,"[9] Oak was enraged and published a booklet in 1893 detailing the shares of himself and others in the *Works*, calling his exposé *"Literary Industries" in a New Light*. The book received little attention at the time; characteristically, it was privately published in a small edition with no public announcement by the author. Oak's only other gesture of proprietorship was to purchase two sets of volumes containing his own writing from the Bancroft firm, which he had bound and labeled the *Works* of Henry L. Oak. He gave one set to his alma mater, Dartmouth, and the other to his brother Ora.[10]

William Nemos, in the statement of 1886, was estimated to have written five volumes, his writings being found in *Central America* I, *Mexico* I–VI, *California* VI–VII, *North Mexican States and Texas* II, and many miscellaneous volumes. His work was conceded to be

---

[7] Nemos, [Notarized statement].

[8] Oak, "Autobiography...."

[9] Bancroft, *Literary Industries*, 568.

[10] Ora's set (11 v.) has been donated to the Bancroft Library by his sons. Contents is in accordance with 1886 statement.

the hardest of all to identify as it was the most scattered, but the last half of *Mexico* I and the first half of *Mexico* II were pointed to as good examples. He shared *California* VI and VII with Bancroft, who characteristically chose to write about the gold discoveries; Mrs. Victor, who wrote on her own specialty, politics; and Oak, who undertook the complicated subject of Mexican land titles.

Nemos was born Knut Gustaf Wilhelm Roos in Stockholm in 1847. His mother was a young unmarried woman of unknown background.[11] Although his nom de plume is derived from the Latin *nemo*, "nobody," with the Swedish genitive affixed, which may indicate that he did not know the identity of his father, he permitted Enrique Cerruti to impress Bancroft with the notion that he was the son of a nobleman. Before joining Bancroft's staff in 1873, he had spent several years in London and visited Australia.[12]

Nemos' talents for organizing research were recognized when he was appointed director of library work and later librarian. In *Literary Industries*, Bancroft praised the talents which fitted Nemos for the position:

> He had a remarkable faculty for systematizing work, and drilling men into a common method, as before explained. Alive to the interests of the library as to his own, he was ever jealous of its reputation, and untiring in his efforts to see produced historical results only of the soundest and most reliable order.[13]

In Nemos' notarized statement of 1889, which he prudently kept to himself until after Bancroft's death in 1918, he also claimed to have engaged and discharged the three grades of workers—indexers, compilers, and advanced writers—and to have apportioned their salaries according to ability, "for Mr. Bancroft rarely interfered in management, owing to frequent and long absences, partly at his store."[14] The letters which Nemos so carefully saved, however, seem to show that he never attempted to hire, or fire or adjust a salary

[11] Gren, *Lychnos*, 49.
[12] Ibid., 49–50.
[13] Bancroft, *Literary Industries*, 255.
[14] Nemos [Notarized statement].

without Bancroft's approval, although Bancroft gave him the power to reduce the force if he saw fit.[15] The removal of the library and literary workshop from the fifth floor of the Market Street building to a specially constructed building on Valencia Street in 1881 did make the direction of both his business and the history more difficult for Bancroft than when they were under the same roof, but he did not surrender control over either.

Nemos did receive permission to use his discretion in specific cases. In 1884 Bancroft placed the fate of one of the indexing and clerical assistants, T. M. Copperthwaite, in the librarian's hands:

> You can do as you think best about letting him go, or paying him $10. or $12½. If he stays he must work. If he wishes to remain long he had better not ask more than $10. as were [sic] are letting men off to reduce expenses and we can easily enough get along without him.[16]

Two excerpts in another letter gave Nemos instructions concerning other assistants:

> ... if Murray continues his short time and hobbies turn him off. He does not deserve the least consideration. And so with Peatfield or any of the rest.... I am tired of this humbug.... You want something definite about Murray—Tell him to put in at least 5 days a week or quit. And to do more work than he has ever done before or quit.[17]

Bancroft appreciated Nemos' efforts to get more work out of his assistants, even when they disagreed on means. In a letter from Mexico in 1883, Bancroft vetoed a suggestion by Nemos concerning salaries:

> I don't believe in rewarding laziness, drunkenness, and incompetency with increased pay, when they are getting more than they are worth already. It is ridiculous taking 18 months to do a Vol. Without any exaggeration, if I was well up in Spanish I would do those Mexican and C. Am pts & biogs at the outside in six months.—that would be only twelve pages a day, & I wouldn't know how to go to work to do less. ... in answer to your sugges-

---

[15] Bancroft to Nemos, November 26, 1884, no. 21.
[16] Bancroft to Nemos, August 20, 1884, no. 4.
[17] Bancroft to Nemos, October 30, 1883, no. 19.

tion of increased pay in certain quarters as a stimulant, I don't think it would work except in the way of bottle stimulant . . . they would not do more and better work for more money.[18]

In the same letter Bancroft made it clear that he was casting no reflection on Nemos, who had done everything that Bancroft could wish: "You have managed everything well I say, and I am under great and lasting obligations to you for it."

Nemos was asked on various occasions to take over every editorial function from planning the order of chapters in the volumes[19] to getting finished manuscript to the printer. In 1883 Bancroft asked him to learn Mexican history in order to preserve the Bancroft reputation:

Mexico, Oct. 30/83

When I consider the immense mass of material on the history of Mexico for the present century, and how much more we shall be criticised during these later years than formerly, and see the men who thoroughl [*sic*] understand themselves and their country—the men here who are to judge us, I am afraid of the work of half sick and drunken men who care only for their Saturday night's pay. Every period requires careful study and intelligent setting forth. I think that some one, yourself for instance, should become thoroughly familiar with all the history from 1800 to 1883 of Mexico and Cent. Am. know every man and every episode by heart, so as to know in going over the MS whether the right view has been taken, and the subject done justice to. Otherwise I am afraid we shall appear ridiculous in the eyes of these Mexicans.[20]

Bancroft was concerned enough about avoiding ridicule to repeat his advice a few days later. After repeating his belief that the history of nineteenth-century Mexico required "brains, time, thought and study" in order to satisfy the Mexican people, he wrote: "They know it by heart and we have got to or else make asses of ourselves."[21] Nemos, of course, applied himself to Mexican history.

[18] Bancroft to Nemos, December 26, 1883, no. 3b.

[19] In a letter from Fort Worth, Texas, Bancroft wrote: "I return your schedule of Cal VI and VII chapters with very few marks on the margin. In fact, I see nothing to criticize. If that is the natural outcome all right; if not, you will change it as occasion requires." Bancroft to Nemos, November, 1885, no. 15.

[20] Bancroft to Nemos, October 30, 1883, no. 19.

[21] Bancroft to Nemos, November 9, 1883, no. 29.

Bancroft sought Nemos' opinion on content, asking him on one occasion what he thought of using three chapters on the Panama Canal to fill the last pages of *Central America* III.[22] In another letter Bancroft confided that he was not happy with the long account of the Modoc War, which was to appear in *California Inter Pocula*: "As you say it is long drawn. If it was not in print I would have it condensed, but it is too late now—that is, it is hardly bad enough to do it all over. Please finish it up briefly & not let the printer be delayed longer than necessary."[23]

Nemos was also consulted on the distribution of work to the writers. In November 1885 Bancroft directed Nemos not to give any part of *California* VI and VII to Alfred Bates,[24] but in April 1886, Bancroft changed his mind and gave Nemos free reign on the distribution of *California* VI, going so far as to suggest: "Bates might do some work on it under you, perhaps, if you would not let him lose a month starting. I think he is doing better work now than ever before." Nemos has added his own note to the letter saying that he did the volume himself except for giving politics to "Mrs. V."[25] Nemos was given the authority to regulate Mrs. Victor's work as early as 1883.[26] Whether he ever had the temerity to do so is doubtful, as Mrs. Victor's letters frequently complain of Bancroft's actions but do not mention Nemos unfavorably.

On at least three occasions, Nemos was invited to revise Bancroft's own work. In a letter written in December of 1884 from Santa Fe, New Mexico, or Omaha, Nebraska (the letterhead carries the names of both cities), Bancroft wrote:

> Do not be afraid of revising my work. It is hastily done—the Soc chapters Diaz, I mean—and needs your finishing thoughts and touches. Please feel at perfect liberty to add, throw out, or rearrange ad libitum, and that you are doing me a kindness, for it is almost impossible for me to do good work of that kind banging about as I am now.[27]

[22] Bancroft to Nemos, October 17, 1885, no. 26b.
[23] Bancroft to Nemos, March 31, 1888, no. 39.
[24] Bancroft to Nemos, November, 1885, no. 15.
[25] Bancroft to Nemos, April 11, 1886, no. 34.
[26] Bancroft to Nemos, October 30, 1883, no. 19.
[27] Bancroft to Nemos, December 9, 1884, no. 14.

"Soc. chapters Diaz" must refer to Chapters VIII–X on Mexican social life and customs in Bancroft's *Life of Porfirio Díaz*. Although the Díaz biography was not part of the *Works*, Bancroft hoped for a wide sale of the book in Mexico. Nemos had studied Mexico, as Bancroft had suggested, and had written passages on the country for the history. In connection with an unspecified work, possibly *California Pastoral*, Nemos was advised to use discretion. Bancroft, stung by derision of his often florid style, wrote his assistant:

> My hifalutin stuff on physical features Cal. won't do. If there is now and then a line from it you can throw in ... with[out] laying ourselves open to the charges of fine writing you can do so. I don't want to give the critics a chance to go for us any more on that score.[28]

Bancroft's letters attest to Nemos' important position in the library, and the estimate of shared authorship prepared by Oak and Nemos credits him with more of the text than any other assistant but Oak. In his affidavit, however, Nemos maintained that he was Bancroft's "sole joint" collaborator on Central America, Mexico, and modern California after the entry of the Americans, as well as on the volumes of the *Works* which followed the *History of the Pacific States*. Nemos also claimed that he, alone of all the assistants, employed subordinate writers to prepare material for his study and re-writing. This, he stated, in addition to his drilling planning, and supervision, "clearly demonstrates my position not alone as chief of staff, but as leading collaborator of Mr. Bancroft and chief contributor and editor."[29] These claims conflict with the Oak-Nemos estimate and indicate that Nemos' desire for recognition blurred his appraisals of the contributions of others.

As Nemos was sensitive enough to keep this statement and all of Bancroft's letters to himself while Bancroft lived, he was one of the small number of Bancroft's business associates who kept up a friendly correspondence with him after leaving his employ.[30] They were much alike in their energy, dedication, and belief in the value

[28] Bancroft to Nemos, November, 1885, no. 15.
[29] Nemos, [Notarized statement].
[30] Bancroft to Nemos, December 6, 1888 and September 7, 1891, nos. –1, 1.

of what they were doing, and, of course, in their drive for recognition. (Nemos gave his collection of Bancroft letters to the Royal Library of Stockholm and occupied much of his time between 1918 and his death in 1933 in correspondence with Swedish libraries, pressing the claims which he had made in the San Francisco statement of 1888.) [31]

Because of Nemos' loyalty and ability, as well as similarity of temperament, he and Bancroft had a warm admiration for each other. Bancroft was dedicated to the history; no matter how much or how little he may have written of it, it was his life's work, and he made friends or enemies of people to the extent that they could appreciate the *Works*. Nemos was proud of his role in the workshop and seemingly content with the recognition he was accorded in *Literary Industries*. Other associates—staff writers, employees of the business, contributors either of data needed to compose or money needed to produce the *Works*, even family members—were often less patient and less admiring, and their relations with Bancroft concluded abruptly and harshly. Among the writers, Oak's bitterness has already been noted. Another of the literary assistants, Frances Fuller Victor, became so incensed at Bancroft's lack of acknowledgment of the true nature of her services that she displayed the four volumes which she had written, *Oregon* I and II, *Washington, Idaho, and Montana*, and *Nevada, Colorado, and Wyoming*, at the San Francisco Winter Fair of 1893. A paper label on the spine identified them as the *Works* of Frances Fuller Victor.[32] She had, of course, already left Bancroft's employ.

Mrs. Victor, the only woman among the writers, was the only assistant with a literary background. As a girl in Ohio, she wrote and published poems with her sister Metta, and, as a young matron in Oregon in 1865, she wrote a society column for two years before publishing two books, *All Over Oregon and Washington* and *The River of the West*. Widowed in 1875, she came to San Francisco and wrote articles for two locally published magazines, the *Golden Era*

[31] Gren, *Lychnos*, 51.
[32] Oak, *"Literary Industries" in a New Light*, 38.

and the *Overland Monthly*. In 1878 she began work for Bancroft.[33] She had begun before her employment to collect material for a history of Oregon, and Bancroft, making good use of her knowledge and contacts, put her to work on his Oregon volumes.

The relation between them on matters touching the *History* was not always smooth, but she worked hard, a quality Bancroft appreciated. He paid tribute in *Literary Industries*: "I have found in Mrs. Frances Fuller Victor, during her arduous labors for a period of ten years in my library, a lady of cultivated mind, of ability and singular application; likewise her physical endurance was remarkable."[34] Mrs. Victor wrote about the physical endurance expected of her in a letter to Elwood Evans: "Last year I wrote or worked fifty-one weeks, every day except Sundays from 8 o'clock in the morning until 6 in the evening, with one hour at noon for exercise and luncheon. This year I am doing the same."[35] For this fifty-four hour week, Mrs. Victor received twenty-three dollars and ten cents,[36] but only Oak and Nemos received more.

Mrs. Victor's work was edited by Bancroft, set up in type, and sent to Judge Matthew P. Deady in Portland. Deady, United States District Court judge for Oregon, read and corrected page proofs for both Oregon volumes at Bancroft's request.[37] Bancroft, of course, hoped to make the history more acceptable to the people of Oregon by this precaution, and Mrs. Victor was apparently agreeable to Deady's participation.

She frequently wrote to the judge concerning her differences with her employer, as she was often disturbed by Bancroft's changes in her work. In one letter she alleged that Bancroft was putting dispar-

[33] Compiled from biographical data in Bancroft, *Literary Industries*, 259–261, and the San Francisco *Chronicle*, May 15, 1881, 1.

[34] Bancroft, *Literary Industries*, 237.

[35] Victor to Evans, January 7, 1880, Western History Collection, Yale University Library.

[36] "Bancroft Library Cash Account, December, 1884–December, 1886." Bancroft Library.

[37] Matthew Paul Deady, "Diary," entry for June 2, 1883. Letters: Bancroft to Deady, March 3, 1886; N. J. Stone to Deady, January 7, 1886. Oregon Historical Society.

aging remarks into the text concerning Orville Pratt, calling him "infamous" and "disgusting" out of malice because Pratt would contribute no material for the history, while being kind to Jessy Thornton, who had dictated at length. The letter continued:

> I happened to know Thornton well enough to weigh his evidence carefully, or whatever he said about being author of the land law, and other misstatements would have gone in more as he desired.... [Bancroft] calls Lane an "Indian butcher" and the like, which is not, as I tell him, historically true, but Lane is dead, and will never buy a set of the histories.[38]

Mrs. Victor told Deady that she was writing about these things, so that he might be on the watch for them when he saw the proofs. "Mr. B. will regard your remarks...."[39]

If Mrs. Victor was unhappy with the manner in which Bancroft's commercial attitudes affected his editing of her work, Bancroft was at least equally unhappy with her initial efforts to write history for him. In a letter to Nemos, he gave her credit for being a good magazine writer and knowing Oregon, but claimed that she could not write history according to "our method," which consisted of a simple story in the text and explanations and discussions in the notes.

> There are whole narratives of leading facts in the notes of which there is no mention in the text, and endless discussion in the text. She does not write to any thread, but seemingly puts down what first comes to her mind, hence she repeats herself over and over. She is inaccurate in her statements and dates. Her deductions are too often from the heart, from her womanly feeling other than from the hard head of the inexorable judge. ... Yet she is a good, honest, talented hard-working woman. What are we to do about it?[40]

Bancroft's solution as expressed in the same letter was to hand the problem to Nemos. Saying that the history of Oregon had to be rewritten, he asked Nemos: "Do you suppose you can make her take

[38] Victor to Deady, June 18, 1883. Oregon Historical Society.
[39] Ibid.
[40] Bancroft to Nemos, [n.d.], no. 10.

her material and by your system or in any way manage to give it to me in proper form?" Bancroft was willing to do one or two of her chapters as a model for Nemos to display, but admitted that he had said nothing to the lady himself. There is no record of how the adjustment was eventually made, but in a later letter Bancroft expresses great satisfaction: "I think Mrs. Victor quite superior in Oregon politics. Perhaps she might do well in Cal. politics though we will not say anything about it at present."[41] Mrs. Victor, of course, is credited by Nemos and Oak with the chapters on politics in *California* VI and VII.

None of the several other assistants who, according to the 1886 statement, contributed a total of nine and one-half volumes to the *Works* made conspicuous attempts to gain public recognition; they have left no record of their reactions to Bancroft or their work. Thomas Savage, in addition to his research activities, wrote *Central America* II, material to the extent of two additional volumes in *Central America* III, *Mexico* III to VI, and miscellaneous other volumes,[42] and an undeterminable portion of *California Pastoral*. J. J. Peatfield, Alfred Bates, T. A. Harcourt, Walter Fisher, and Ivan Petroff each contributed one-half to two volumes of the finished work. There were also writers employed in the early days of the production of the *Native Races* whose writing was almost entirely revised by the others.[43] Little of this revision was done by Bancroft.

The claims of the literary assistants for recognition as authors of the *Works* are purely ethical, as Bancroft had the legal right to present the work of writers whom he had hired without specifically acknowledging their contributions. Oak admits as much in his account of the workshop. In defense of his exposé, he continues:

But I insist . . . that if Mr. Bancroft saw fit to take the public into his confidence, in a deliberate and detailed exposition of his "literary industries," he was bound to make that exposition absolutely truthful . . . that five volumes out of a total of thirty-three formed too slight a basis for his

[41] Bancroft to Nemos, July 26, 188—, no. 24.
[42] Oak and Nemos, "Estimate. . . ."
[43] Ibid.

exclusive claims; that twenty-eight volumes were quite enough to merit some credit for the writers *as writers* . . . .[44]

Oak's argument is difficult to answer; it is also difficult to believe that Bancroft recognized that planning a work, allotting research and writing, and revising proof on the results did not constitute authorship. Neither his published writings, nor his letters give evidence of it.

[44] Oak, *"Literary Industries" in a New Light*, 53.

Chapter IV

THE INTRODUCTION OF THE *NATIVE RACES*

LONG BEFORE Bancroft and his literary assistants recognized that the method of writing begun with the *Native Races* was to obtain throughout the remainder of the *Works*, text was going into print. Composition on volume I was begun in May 1873.[1] Although it was to be fourteen months before the composition was completed and the volume in print, Bancroft and his business staff had to plan methods to bring his work to the attention of the public. The projected work and the library from which it sprang were unique and impressive; newspaper and magazine editors might give them notice if it were made easy for them to do so.

Editors frequently welcome "fillers," items which may range from two lines of type to six or more column inches, and which retain whatever interest they may have for the reader over a long period of time. Once received by the editor, they may be held until needed to complete the make-up of a page. All publishers know this, and most of them supply newspapers with information on books and authors suitable for this purpose.

Bancroft was familiar with the practice, and, realizing in the first months of 1874 that he would be able to publish the first volume of the *Native Races* within the year, he released feature length articles

[1] Hubert Howe Bancroft, "Composition Costs and Printing Information concerning the *Native Races*" (handwritten), 1, [History Company Records].

and short fillers on the library and some of the special collections in it. The response was only moderately satisfactory. Newspapers from Sonoma to Monterey including the metropolitan dailies of San Francisco were cooperative, and a few New York papers ran articles, but notices appearing in California and elsewhere in 1874 were generally brief. With the possible exception of an eight-page article in the *Overland Monthly* of June 1874 signed by Henry Oak, information about Bancroft and his work appearing before August 1874 could easily have been overlooked by prospective subscribers.[2]

Bancroft solicited and received letters from several western authors, including J. Ross Browne, writer and authority on Indians of the Southwest, where he had served as United States Treasury Agent, and Frederick Whymper, who had written a work on Alaska. Browne's and Whymper's letters were exceedingly friendly and lavish in their praise. Both writers were familiar with a few of Bancroft's "Wild Tribes" and their tributes show that volume I had been well done. Browne stated:

> The tribes best known to me are the Apaches, Pimas, Maricopas and Yumas of Arizona. Not a single incorrect or unsupported statement occurs in your work, so far as my knowledge intends respecting these tribes. The style in which you have presented their peculiarities of character, their customs and traditions is clear, simple and attractive.... Such works as you have undertaken and so happily accomplished as far as you have gone, are not for today or tomorrow, but for all time.... The honorable distinction to which you aspire, as the builder of an edifice that may be useful to all mankind, from scattered materials that would otherwise have been lost or unavailable; a receptacle of data from which the student or historian may draw at pleasure is well merited by your fidelity to truth, the unselfish sacrifice of your private means and the intrinsic value of your work....[3]

Mr. Whymper's letter, though briefer and more careful to avoid

[2] "Notices and Reviews of the Library and of the 'Native Races of the Pacific States,'" (Scrapbook), Bancroft Library. Bancroft and members of his staff kept scrapbooks of notices which were published concerning the collections, the library, and the *Works*. The notices and reviews of the *Native Races* fill two and one-half volumes and include items obviously sent out by the Bancroft office as well as reviews.

[3] Browne to Bancroft, June 19, 1874, [History Company Records].

entangling metaphors, was no less enthusiastic:

> After inspecting the proof sheets of the first volume of your grand work on "The Native Races of the Pacific States," I am firmly convinced that it will make one of the most valuable additions to ethnological science ever issued from the press of any country.... In regard to the natives of Alaska, a subject which in the course of my wanderings I became somewhat familiar, I see that you have put together in a complete mosaic all the information possibly attainable at the present time.[4]

Bancroft printed portions of these letters as well as other bouquets in a circular which finally reached sixteen pages of flattering testimonials,[5] but he needed even bigger names before facing the critics.

In the late nineteenth century, most of the arbiters of American literary taste lived in or near Boston. If Bancroft could gain their approval, his work was almost certain to be a critical success—and critical approbation was vital to insure a wide sale for the *Native Races*. According to his own admission, Bancroft was proud and sensitive. He did not look forward to displaying his work to strangers, but he could not afford to be ignored; therefore, he resolved to present copies of his first book to the New England writers and ask them their opinion of it.[6]

Bancroft went east in August 1874 with several sets of the printed sheets for volume I and for parts of later volumes in his trunk. The plates for the volume, which had been composed and made up in San Francisco, had been shipped to New York, as Bancroft believed that a leading publisher's name would help the work's reception, and he intended to find one.

When he arrived in New York City on August 14, he went first to Harper and Brothers, the firm which had published William Hickling Prescott's popular and highly regarded *Conquest of Mexico*. Joseph Abner Harper talked to him briefly but assured him that John Wesley Harper was the proper person to see, and that the latter was at the seaside. Bancroft was turned over to a Mr. Connant, "a

---

[4] Whymper to Bancroft, June 11, 1874, [History Company Records].
[5] Bancroft, *Literary Industries*, 313.
[6] Ibid., 317–319.

cold cynical cuss," whose attitude discomfited the author. Connant, after keeping Bancroft waiting while he officiously went through some routine work, listened briefly to the historian's plans and an account of his literary methods. As the proper Harper was not to return to the office for a week, Bancroft left a copy of the book with Connant, who promised to look it over.[7]

Bancroft visited relatives in Buffalo over the weekend immediately following, but was too restless to remain with them until Harper should return. On Monday he went to New Haven, only to find almost all of the professors away for the summer. At the railway station he encountered President Daniel Coit Gilman of the University of California, and Gilman invited Bancroft to a conference of the American Scientific Association in Hartford.[8]

In Hartford Gilman introduced him to Charles Dudley Warner, editor of the Hartford *Courant*, and both men gave him letters of introduction to other savants. Armed with these letters and enheartened by Warner's warm approval, Bancroft set out to call on most of the leading literary figures of the day.[9]

He took with him Porter C. Bliss, whom he had met at the convention at Hartford. Bliss was an authority on genealogy and the owner of a library on Mexico which he planned to sell. Bancroft wanted first chance at the library, and he hoped that Bliss, by his presence and easy conversation, would cover some of his own diffidence and nervousness. As the journey proceeded, however, Bancroft became more confident of himself and irked by his companion. In recollection, he made Bliss an entirely ridiculous figure.

Although Bancroft had intended to ask eastern scholars to examine the book and give an immediate opinion of it in writing, he was dissuaded from so flat a demand by one of those whom he saw first, Dr.

[7] Hubert Howe Bancroft, "Personal Observations during a Tour through the Line of Missions in Upper California," 1874 (?) (handwritten), 187–188. Bancroft Library. The account of Bancroft's eastern journey follows the story of the California travels.

[8] Ibid., 189–190.

[9] Bancroft, *Literary Industries*, 331–332. The account in the book (pp. 328–340) is more detailed than that in the journal, but the printed narrative omits the encounter with Harper and Brothers.

Asa Gray, of Harvard. Gray suggested that he let these opinions come as they would in good time, and not try to force them out immediately in order to send them to book reviewers. Bancroft wanted to influence the reviews, but he needed approbation and realized that some of the savants would be reluctant to deliver it on demand. Dr. Gray gave him letters to Francis Parkman, Charles Francis Adams, and others.

Bancroft was generally cordially received. He called on Lowell, who listened attentively and directed a warm letter of approval to San Francisco after he had had time to read the volume. Wendell Philips greeted Bancroft with enthusiasm and gave him a letter to Phillips' friend, Whittier. Whittier gave him letters to Longfellow and Emerson, remarking in his letter to Longfellow: "What materials for poems will be gathered up in these volumes! It seems to me one of the noblest literary enterprises of our day." Bancroft agreed to deliver the Longfellow letter if he were permitted to retain it. He failed to find Longfellow, though he sought him at the poet's summer and winter homes but he eventually established contact by mail.

Emerson's reception of Bancroft and Bliss was polite but cool, and, though Bliss thawed the essayist by a display of his exhaustive knowledge of genealogy, Bancroft was impatient with both of them: "In my present frame of mind I was quite ready to quarrel with any person whose hobby came in conflict with my hobby, or who did not regard my efforts with the consideration I thought they deserved. I was possessed of an idea."[10]

When Bancroft visited Charles Francis Adams, the latter suggested that if Bancroft could get Francis Parkman to review his book for the *North American Review*, "it would be a great thing for it." Bancroft sought Parkman out and found him receptive and agreeable to reviewing the book on its merits although the older historian admitted that he might not be equipped to do the subject justice. Bancroft, of course, was delighted to have the promise of a review in a leading American journal from a historian of Parkman's stature.

In Cambridge William Dean Howells agreed to place a ten-page

10 Ibid., 339.

review in the *Atlantic Monthly*, a review originally allotted to Bliss but passing by default, much to Bancroft's pleasure, to Clarence King, a brilliant young scientist, soon to be founding-head of the United States Geological Survey. Although Bancroft missed personal interviews with Oliver Wendell Holmes and Edward Everett Hale, both men wrote him letters from which flattering phrases could be excerpted.[11]

Between visits with celebrities, Bancroft made his business arrangements. From the staff of the Riverside Press, he obtained a satisfactory estimate on printing and binding; prices being set at 90 cents for each volume in cloth binding, and $1.35 for sheepskin.[12] Plates were forwarded, and three thousand sets in three printings were completed there, "being followed by other thousands."[13]

Bancroft returned to Harper but was unable to come to terms concerning publishing. In an unpublished journal he recorded the consequences:

> When I first came on [*sic*] I went to J. C. Derby an old friend and brother of Geo. H. Derby in whose employ I was brought up to the business— Mr. J. C. Derby now has charge of the subscription dept. of D. Appleton & Co. I left him a copy of the book and asked him to tell me what was the best I could do with it. Naturally enough he advised me to place it in the hands of some strong house, Appleton's for instance, and have it sold by subscription. I was not partial to this way of working it at first but by degrees I came to regard it more favorably. So that in talking the matter over with Harper he was so unreasonable about it that I concluded to let Appleton have it.[14]

On September 23,[15] arrangements were completed for publication of his work with Appleton. Bancroft was to furnish the books printed and bound, and Appleton was to account for them at one-half retail prices. The contract was for five years.[16]

[11] Ibid., 339–340, 350.
[12] Bancroft, "Personal Observations ...," 193.
[13] Bancroft, *Literary Industries*, 336.
[14] Bancroft, "Personal Observations ...," 200.
[15] Ibid., 201.
[16] Bancroft, *Literary Industries*, 346.

Publication in London was given to Longmans, in Paris, to Maisonneuve et Cie, and in Leipzig, to F. A. Brockhaus. French and German publishers assured Bancroft that they would place reviews in the leading periodicals of their countries. From Longmans, author's copies were sent to Herbert Spencer, Thomas Carlyle, Thomas Huxley, William Lecky, Edward Tylor, and several other prominent scientists and historians, most of whom responded generously.

Spencer was most grateful, writing Bancroft that he wished that the entire five volumes were available, as they would have assisted in the preparation of "tabular statements and extracts" for Spencer's own work, *Descriptive Sociology*. The letter then expressed the hope that Professor Duncan, one of Spencer's own literary assistants, would be able to use information from Bancroft's work while the division of *Descriptive Sociology* dealing with the American races was passing through the press. Spencer closed his note with thanks to Bancroft for "sympathy not remaining passive, but becoming active as a stimulus and guide to research."[17] Letters like this were as good as formal reviews, and Bancroft released them to western papers.

Upon his return to San Francisco Bancroft asked President Gilman, also returned from the eastern states, to review his book for the *Overland Monthly*. Gilman was to be furnished with material written by Oak, Nemos, and T. A. Harcourt and Walter Fisher, two young men who had left Bancroft's employment to take over editorship of the *Overland*. Bancroft states that the material was given to the professor in November, and the review wanted for the December issue, yet Gilman was to "verify every statement, make thorough personal investigation, and speak with dignity and decision concerning the work, commending or condemning, as his judgment might dictate." No one should have known better than Bancroft the impossibility of a busy administrator's accomplishing so great a task in so short a time, but when Harcourt came in with the review, Bancroft was appalled. Gilman had written a summary of what he

---

[17] Spencer to Bancroft, February, 1875. Entire letter printed Sacramento *Daily Union* and Sacramento *Daily Record*, March 13, 1875.

had been told, giving due credit for every piece of information: "Mr. Nemos says this, Mr. Goldschmidt that, Mr. Harcourt the other thing." Bancroft attributed the scholar's reluctance to praise an unfamiliar work to timidity, and tore up the review.[18]

Harcourt was sent to get a notice to take its place from J. Ross Browne, whose friendliness was already evident from the letter he had written earlier. Bancroft termed the review appearing in the December 1884 *Overland* over Browne's name, "one of the best articles ever written on the subject."[19] Henry Oak alleged that he [Oak] wrote it.[20] As very limited time remained in which to write a review and Browne had expressed friendliness towards the book, he was probably willing enough to lend the prestige of his name to the sort of review Bancroft wanted and Oak was equipped to produce.

The ten-page article appearing in the *Overland*[21] contains much information on Bancroft's methods and almost nothing on the content of the volume. There are no references to the tribes of Indians Browne knew, and, in contrast to the enthusiasm of Browne's letter, the review is flat, formal, pompous, and dull. It was, however, designed to impress the reader with the care and erudition that would go into every volume, and, as such, served Bancroft better than an effusion over the single volume would have done.

As well as soliciting the *Overland Monthly* review, Bancroft, on his return from the East, "set out and made a thorough canvass of the papers in San Francisco and obtained from them flattering preliminary notices, as well as reviews of the work when it was out."[22] The appearance of the *Overland* review was followed by notices from other California and western papers and a few on the Atlantic seaboard and in the Midwest. Although a review in the Sacramento *Record* of January 1, 1875, devotes an entire page to Bancroft, the library, and the *Native Races*, most notices are fillers or brief reviews. Some are reprints of the *Overland* article or other reviews; others

[18] Bancroft, *Literary Industries*, 321–323.
[19] Ibid., 323.
[20] Oak, *"Literary Industries" in a New Light*, 57.
[21] *Overland Monthly*, XIII (December, 1874), 551–560.
[22] Bancroft, "Personal Observations . . . ," 203.

read as if they had been prepared by the Bancroft staff.[23]

An article in the Vallejo *Chronicle* of February 19 tried to help sales by advocating support of the work for material reasons. The article maintained that the history would attract people and money to California: "Every man who holds an interest on this coast to the amount of $500 should support Mr. Bancroft in his work, for he is taking the surest, quickest and most direct means of any to double that $500 that it is possible to employ." Although this cannot have displeased Bancroft and his sales staff, the idea may well have been the Vallejo editor's own, as the promotion continually stressed the historical importance and cultural value of Bancroft's endeavors, as well as the alleged interest to the reader of their result, and carried no implication of material returns.

Eastern and midwestern reviews began to appear in late December. Periodicals and newspapers from Boston to Chicago were generous with approval, although Bancroft's literary style was criticized in a few articles. The New York *World* strongly criticized the author for confusing his readers with contradictory footnotes, but other reviewers recognized the value of Bancroft's comprehensiveness.

The review which Bancroft had sought from Francis Parkman must have satisfied his highest expectations. Parkman, writing in the *North American Review* for January 1875 found space in the course of a thirteen-page laudatory appreciation of the *Native Races* to express his approval of the official version of the Bancroft method:

> The volume now before us was written with the aid of a corps of fellow-laborers, who, judging from the results were exceedingly well chosen.... All acted together in pursuance of plans developed by Mr. Bancroft, who followed them with critical supervision, testing their work by comparison with original sources, and giving form and character to the whole. If this method has its objections, it is certain that no one man could accomplish the proposed task by any other.

The review devotes about ten pages to the content of the volume,

[23] Notices cited and summarized in this chapter, unless otherwise identified, may be found in "Notices and Reviews of the Library and of the 'Native Races of the Pacific States.'" Bancroft Library.

then concludes with the sentence: "A literary enterprise more deserving of generous sympathy and support has never been undertaken on this side of the Atlantic."[24]

Bancroft's letter expressing his gratitude to Parkman has been preserved and displays in two short pages the blend of business sense, the simple pleasure in the good opinion of the learned world, and the devotion to work which drove him to completion of his projected series of histories and shaped his campaign to sell them. Bancroft wrote:

My dear Mr. Parkman

   I thank you a thousand times for your very full and flattering review of my book. The good it will do me it is hard to overestimate. In view of a prospective twenty years or so work in one direction you can imagine something of what it is to have a square understanding with the world at the start, especially when it is so favorable to me—when those whose opinion I most prize are so ready to give me greater praise at the beginning than I had ever dared to hope would be mine at the end of my career.

   Now I am satisfied; and I can let fame rest for awhile and turn my whole thoughts to doing good and thorough work.

   Holding myself ever in readiness to serve you to the full extent of my ability, and thanking you once more

   I am very sincerely yours

San Fran   Jan 17/75   H H Bancroft[25]

In September 1875 Bancroft, feeling perhaps that he had let fame rest long enough, wrote again to Parkman to request: "If you will do me the favor to look a little after the review in the *North American* you will add to the deep obligation I am already under to you."[26] Parkman's reply has not been preserved, but a review of volumes two, three, and four of *Native Races* duly appeared in the *North American Review* for October, 1875. The review is brief, considering all three volumes within eight pages. Although it is unsigned, the editorial "we" used in referring to the first review, and a state-

[24] Quotations from: Francis Parkman, "The Native Races of the Pacific States," *North American Review*, CXX (January, 1875), 36, 47.

[25] Bancroft to Parkman, January 17, 1875. Massachusetts Historical Society.

[26] Bancroft to Parkman, September 25, 1875. Massachusetts Historical Society.

ment in a letter from Parkman to Oliver Wendell Holmes ("I reviewed some of his early vols. but have no time to do more.") indicate that Parkman wrote it.[27]

Clarence King, although he was occupied with preparing his own impressive work, the *Report of the Geological Exploration of the Fortieth Parallel, 1870–1880*, took time to write a cordial ten-page review in the *Atlantic Monthly*, which makes the content of *Native Races* I sound absorbing. He took no notice of Bancroft's historical method, and his concluding paragraph reads as if he had not been briefed on the subject:

> It is not a little noteworthy that so monumental a literary labor should have been accomplished in a new country, far from all scholastic atmosphere, remote from the daily association with fellow investigators by the perseverance of one courageous student.[28]

Bancroft's reply to this tribute has not been located.

Foreign reviews, although relatively few in number, were almost always generous, long articles appearing in the *Times*, the *Academy* (London), and the *Westminster Review*. These most influential reviews appeared in March and April 1875; the scrapbooks which Bancroft preserved for his children contain shorter English reviews which preceded them, and a few French and German notices. A long review appearing in the *Revue Politique et Libraire* concludes: It has the comfortable typography of an English publication, it is stuffed with facts like a German encyclopedia, it is as methodical and enlightened as a French book.[29]

Bancroft's own statement seems thoroughly justified: "Never probably was a book so generally and so favorably reviewed by the best journals in Europe and America. Never was an author more suddenly and more thoroughly brought to attention of learned and

---

[27] *North American Review*, CXXI (October, 1875), 442–450; Parkman to Holmes, Boston, May 28 [year conjectural] in: Francis Parkman, *Letters* ... edited and with an introduction by Wilbur R. Jacobs (Norman: University of Oklahoma Press, [c. 1960]), v. ii, 151.

[28] Clarence King, "Bancroft's Native Races of the Pacific States," *Atlantic Monthly*, XXV (February, 1875), 173.

[29] My translation of a clipping from: *Revue Politique et Libraire*, June 5, 1875.

literary men everywhere."[30] He would probably not have achieved so much had he candidly stated: "Here is the first volume of a five-volume anthropological, archeological, and historical work which some bright young men are writing from source works in my remarkable library, according to a plan I have set down for them." Bancroft, the publisher, knew that an unknown author was difficult enough to introduce to the world of learning; an acknowledged compilation by a variety of unknown hands would have been impossible. Bancroft's assumption of the praise and honors that were showered upon him for the *Native Races*, however, made it impossible for him to back down publicly on the issue of authorship of any of his works. As a publisher, he needed to use and reuse the endorsements he had worked so hard to win.

[30] Bancroft, *Literary Industries*, 361.

CHAPTER V

THE BEGINNING OF THE CAMPAIGN

IN 1874 BANCROFT had a flourishing subscription department. When he confessed himself "not partial" to having his books sold by this method, he may have done so because of the poor repute into which subscription publishing had fallen. From the fifteenth century onward, subscriptions or pledges had been solicited from prospective purchasers in advance of printing certain expensive works. The practice gave publishers sufficient capital to bring out works of doubtful mass appeal but some merit. In nineteenth-century America, however, subscriptions were often taken for published works having great potential mass appeal in order to assure huge sales. These sales were handled by canvassers, carrying prospectuses and order blanks rather than books.

Sales manuals for book agents show that canvassers were coached by publishers in aggressive sales techniques, stressing appeals to the prospect's vanity, ambition, and aspirations for his children. The surviving manuals are markedly similar in demonstrating that adroit manipulation of the samples of text, illustration, and binding in the prospectus, impressive presentation of a locally eminent list of subscribers, and an unfaltering delivery of a memorized sales talk were far more important to the canvasser in gaining orders than the intrinsic merit of his wares.[1]

Many patrons did not like what they got for their money, even though subscription works were usually at least six hundred pages in length to justify the high prices asked for them.[2] The book trade stressed these discontents in its abuse of the canvasser, who was hurting business, as publishers tended to sell some of their most popular titles in this way.[3]

For the personal canvass did succeed in selling books. It was particularly appropriate for sets—long histories, encyclopedias, and collected works—as time-payment plans could be devised to put multi-volume publications within reach of persons of modest means. The *New American Cyclopedia*, the *Encyclopaedia Britannica*, and Guizot's *Popular History of France*, as well as many other sets, had all done well through subscription sales.

The *New American Cyclopedia* had been published by Appleton in sixteen volumes between 1857 and 1863. "Tens of thousands" of sets of the original edition had been sold, and a revised illustrated edition, published in 1872, was selling rapidly at the time Bancroft visited the firm.[4] Derby can hardly have failed to have mentioned this success, and Bancroft, who wanted to sell the *Native Races* to

[1] Seven surviving manuals are: *The Book Agent: A Manual of Confidential Instructions; Unfolding in Detail and in a Thoroughly Practical Manner, the Best Methods of Conducting the Business of Canvassing....* (San Francisco: A. L. Bancroft, [18_]) [imprint is a pasted cancelans] 61 pp.; [W. S. Bryan] *A Friendly Talk with the Agent,* [n.p., c. 1888, 1892] 58 pp.; *Helpful Hints, or How to Become a Successful Agent* (Chicago, 1887), reprinted in Hamlin Hill, *Mark Twain and Elisha Bliss* (Columbia: University of Missouri Press, [c. 1964]), 170–182; *Key: How to Introduce the Personal Memoirs of U. S. Grant; Description of the Prospectus* ([n.p.] R. S. Peale, 1885), 37 pp.; *O. A. Browning's Confidential Instructions; Rules and Helps for his Agents, Embracing a Complete Description of the Book Agency Business....* (Toledo, Ohio, 1881), 94 pp.; Henry B. Scammell, *Principles and Practice of Successful Book Canvassing in Brief* (St. Louis, [1878]), 12 pp.; *Strictly Private. Henry Bill's Confidential Directions to his Agents for Selling his Books by Subscription* (Norwich, Conn., [c. 1878]), 27 pp.

[2] Hill, *Mark Twain and Elisha Bliss*, 13.

[3] *Publishers' Weekly,* XV (March 8, 1879), 279; XVII (April 24, 1880), 425; XIX (May 7, 1881), 510; 548–549.

[4] Grant Overton, *Portrait of a Publisher ... and The First Hundred Years of the House of Appleton, 1825–1925* (New York: Appleton, 1925), 6, 45.

John Dewey Library
Johnson State College
Johnson, Vermont

the general public as well as to collectors, libraries, and other historians, must have been impressed by the sales record.

There were several arguments for selling Bancroft's own work by subscription. Canvassers could persuade patrons to sign contracts to pay for the books as published. The price per volume for the *Native Races*, originally set at $5.50 for cloth and $6.00 for sheepskin in the West, with other bindings priced in proporton, was much less formidable than $27.50, $30.00, or more for the complete set. As an early advertisement phrased it: "By subscribing for this work *now*, it is secured on the very small cost of the price of one volume, once per quarter, which in cloth or sheep, can be met by a saving of less than ten cents per day."[5]

This installment plan was designed to help the publisher as well as the reader. Bancroft hoped to be able, by receiving payments for each volume as it was sold, to meet the cost of later volumes with proceeds from earlier ones. His ability to continue his work without great financial loss depended on the sale of the anthropological volumes, as some of their seventy-thousand-dollar cost had to be realized before the historical works could be issued.[6]

The nature of the territory in which Bancroft hoped to arouse the most interest in the set presented another argument in favor of canvassing. California and the other "Pacific" states were predominantly rural and agricultural. Despite the presence of numerous small-town bookstores, many farmers and ranchers were not "readers." Bancroft wanted to reach this group as well as more sophisticated people who did patronize bookstores habitually. A house-to-house canvass could introduce his book to the audiences he sought.

[5] "Why the Public should avail themselves of the earliest possible opportunity to secure the great Pacific Coast Work, The Native Races of the Pacific States, which is sold only by Subscription, at $5.50 per volume in cloth, and $6.00 do. in sheep." Single sheet advertisement in "Notices and Reviews of the Library and of the 'Native Races of the Pacific States.' "

Appleton agents in the East offered the volume at $5.50 cloth and $6.50 in sheep. This would have been the retail price on which Bancroft's half-share was computed. Eastern agents' advertisements are pasted among the last leaves in "Notices and Reviews of the Library and of the 'Native Races of the Pacific States.' "

[6] Ibid.

Finally, Bancroft could, with the letters and reviews he had solicited in advance of publication, present his work as a public benefit. Subscribers for books published in eighteenth-century England had been made to feel that they were patrons of learning in order to gain their financial support. Bancroft, with the letters he had received from Whittier, Lowell, Oliver Wendell Holmes, and other eminent men, had material with which to attempt such an appeal. In a manual published for canvassers for the *Native Races*, the agents were exhorted to tell prospective subscribers:

> It is a great work that he [Bancroft] is doing, and he wants every good intelligent man on the coast to know about it, and appreciate it and take an interest in it. . . .

> I want you to believe in this important work, to believe that it is a good work, good for the country and every man in it, and that it has been well done.[7]

The nature of the book could have been the ultimate argument. There is no strong narrative thread to hold a reader who might glance at the work in the bookstore. The first volume is almost a catalog of individual tribes and customs. The subject was not of great current interest—even the "author" found it repulsive. These factors would have told heavily against bookstore sale. To a canvasser, they were almost irrelevant. A skillfully made prospectus could present all the most interesting passages in the book, and the agent would accent these to make the volume sound absorbing. The work did have the one thing essential in any subscription book, bulk. Subscribers expected a lot of text for their money, and each of Bancroft's volumes was to be eight hundred pages long.

Bancroft took the western agency for the *Native Races*, but he inaugurated no radical changes in canvassing techniques in the campaign to sell the work. The manual for the five-volume set, [*Strictly Private.*] *How Properly to Place Hubert Bancroft, His Library, and*

7 [*Strictly Private.*] *How Properly to Place Hubert Bancroft, his Library, and his Work Before Every Intelligent Man on the Pacific Coast,* [San Francisco: A. L. Bancroft, 1874 (?)], 4, 13, in "Scrapbook of Materials about Hubert Howe Bancroft, his Works, and the Bancroft Library."

His Works Before Every Intelligent Man on the Pacific Coast, is relatively brief, as another manual was given to the new agent in order to help him learn the general practices of canvassing.[8]

The agent for the *Native Races* was urged to come to San Francisco before beginning work. He was to go to the second floor of A. L. Bancroft and Company and call on Theodore C. Smith, head of the subscription division. Smith would take him to visit the library, where, the training manual said, Bancroft [!] or one of the assistants would go over the work with the neophyte before taking him around the fifth floor to observe the assistants at their labors.[9] Suitably awed by the magnitude of Bancroft's endeavor, the canvasser would next study his prospectus and his book (*Native Races* I) for a week or two, memorizing an eleven-page "Description" which forms the greater part of [*Strictly Private.*].

This speech, to be delivered to prospects after a few initial remarks had established rapport, mentions Bancroft's collections, his withdrawal from business, his use of assistants in preparing material for his writing, and draws attention to some of the authorities used in the volumes offered. The agent was to produce his prospectus, point out these authorities, and then guide his listener through the pages, emphasizing the time invested in writing text and notes, and the reliability of the information therein. Instructions for this presentation call attention to portions of the text that might interest readers, but the main theme is stressed again and again: this is the truth about the American Indians, and only Bancroft has the sources from which it can be written.[10]

After going through the prospectus, the canvasser was instructed to display copies of some of the letters of praise which Bancroft had received, and to read a few quotations. After this ritual, which took the place of the display of the subscription list in general canvassing routine, the canvasser was to: *"read the conditions clearly and emphatically, at the same time handing your pen or pencil to the reader as though he would subscribe as a matter of course."* If this action

[8] [*Strictly Private.*], 1.
[9] Ibid., 1–2.
[10] Ibid., 4–14.

failed to get a signature, the agent was to persist in his arguments. When there was no more hope of an immediate order, the agent assured the prospect that he would receive further news of the progress of Bancroft's work, invited the man to visit the Bancroft company when he was in San Francisco, and bid him goodbye.[11]

The procedure is the same as that described earlier in the chapter, but there were two variations on the basic formula for all canvassing presentations. One was the above-mentioned appeal for patronage, which falls at the beginning and at the close of the agent's presentation; the other was an appeal to vanity, occurring about one-fourth of the way through. The agent was to say:

> Mr. Bancroft is still collecting everything he can lay his hands on. If you, or any of your friends, can give him anything on the history of the coast, you will be doing him a great favor, and the country a lasting benefit. Besides you can here place yourself, and any facts in your possession properly before the world. The early settlers are dying off, and an immense amount of valuable information dies with every one of them. What a magnificent work it is to rescue from oblivion so much that would otherwise be forever lost. And this is what Mr. Bancroft is doing, and he wants you and every other high-minded, intelligent man to do what you can towards it.[12]

The plea for patronage and the plea for information must have been Bancroft's own ideas, as they figure in his own activities and correspondence. He quite sincerely saw himself as conserver of the heritage of the past, and he felt his efforts deserved support. However, this long-winded speech for the *Native Races*, which is filled with italicized directions for actions on the part of the agent, gives no indication that the canvasser should pause after asking for information, and no instructions on how to take down any data given to him. The request for "facts in your posssession" seems to have been a mere gesture at this time, but it was to become one of the most distinctive features of the canvass for the complete *Works*.

If the canvasser were successful, his subscriber signed a contract agreeing to pay for the volumes as received. As the set was sent di-

11 Ibid., 13–14.
12 Ibid., 1–2.

rectly to subscribers by mail or express,[13] canvassers were freed from the usual burden of buying volumes from the publisher, storing, and delivering them. The agent need only purchase his "outfit" of prospectus and order blanks, study hard, go to his territory, and sell books.

Canvassers were promised $10 per subscriber which amounts to 36 percent of the retail price ($27.50) of the set in cloth binding.[14] The percentage is not high in proportion to the cost of the entire work, but it could be earned by making only one presentation. Canvassers attracted by these terms succeeded in selling over three thousand sets.[15]

The first volume of the *Native Races*, subtitled *Wild Tribes*, was published on December 1, 1874. Volume II, *Civilized Nations*, was published in May 1875, and volumes III–V, *Myths and Languages*, *Antiquities*, and *Primitive History* followed at quarterly intervals.

Bancroft had devoted considerable thought to the physical appearance of his volumes:

Matters of no inconsiderable importance and care with me were the type I should use and the style of my page. After examining every variety within my reach, I settled on the octavo English edition of Buckle's *Civilization*, as well for the text and notes as for the system of numbering the notes from the beginning to the end of the chapter. It was plain, broad-faced, clear and beautiful, and easily read. The notes and reference figures were all in perfect

[13] The mode of delivery is not set down in canvassers' manuals. However, canvassers' memoranda to Nathan Stone, e.g., J'no. Lang to Stone, February 28, 1888, and L. S. Hatch to Stone, July 18, 1888, indicate that the agents did not make deliveries. E. B. Colwell to Stone, April 18, 1889, mentions, in a note accompanying an order for the *Works*, that: "The book case is to be sent with the books to Meridian [California]...." All letters in [History Company Records]. A. E. Parsons to J. B. Colton, April 30, 1884, states: "The books are sent postage paid." Henry E. Huntington Library, San Marino, California.

[14] (*Confidential*), [printed brochure for prospective canvassers]. In: "Scrapbook of Materials about Hubert Howe Bancroft, his Works, and the Bancroft Library." Bancroft Library. There is no indication of whether "$100 for 10 subscribers" (the phrase in the pamphlet) is based on cloth binding commission, full morocco binding commission, or a reasonable average. All canvassers would expect to receive more commission for selling more expensive bindings.

[15] Bancroft, *Literary Industries*, 336.

taste and harmony.... I sent to Scotland for the type, as I could find none of it in America.[16]

The results of this decision may be observed in the Appleton edition of the *Native Races*. The volumes are demy-octavos—page size 6 by 9 inches untrimmed. The paper is medium weight, creamy white, and lightly glazed. Although machine-made, it is of good quality and, after nearly a century, shows no signs of foxing or brittleness.

The text is set in 12 point modern face type, unleaded, with copious footnotes in 8 point. The face appears identical to one which the American Type Founders Company featured as "Roman no. 10" in their *Pacific Coast Blue Book* of 1896.[17] Half-title and title pages are set in capitals of the same font in various sizes with a generous use of white space. On the recto of the following page of volume I, are the words: "TO/ MY BROTHER/ ALBERT L. BANCROFT/ I DEDICATE THIS WORK."

Pages vii to xiii of volume I contain the preface to the work, which explains the choice and limitation of subject matter, before discussing the library, and the author's use of assistants in historical research. The concluding sentence acknowledges the assistance of T. Arundel-Harcourt [*sic*] in gathering material for the history of the civilized nations [Aztecs, Mayas, etc.], Walter Fisher for the same services in mythology, Albert Goldschmidt in languages, and Henry Oak in antiquities and aboriginal history.

There are several maps in the *Native Races*, as there are in many volumes of the *History of the Pacific States*. Bancroft had built up a wide clientele for his excellent maps of the western states, and he did not intend to disappoint purchasers of the *Works*. Cultural areas, exploration routes, immigration trails, battlegrounds, and settlements could be easily charted using plates in Bancroft's stock for reference.

Only one volume of the entire *Works* could be called illustrated.

[16] Bancroft, *Literary Industries*, 569–570.

[17] Comparison and measurement made by writer with specimens in American Type Founders Company, *Pacific Coast Blue Book* (San Francisco, 1896), 164, 169. The face has marked thick-thin contrast with heavy vertical lines characteristic of modern types. The serifs are sturdy, however, rather than hairline and are slightly bracketed.

Many volumes are without illustrations of any kind, a few contain
one or two cuts, but *Native Races* IV, *Antiquities*, has over four
hundred wood engravings. Picturing varied objects, from potsherds
to monolithic idols and temples, the cuts range from one inch square
or less, to full-page size. Bancroft acknowledged in the preface to
the volume that he had obtained many woodcuts which had first
been printed in the works of E. G. Squier and John L. Stephens.[18]
Squier and Stephens had both published lavishly illustrated books on
Central America some years before.[19] Bancroft also had cuts engraved from lithographs in Stephens' work and from other sources.
In no other volume were pictures so vital to the text, and the author
made little further effort to secure them.

After the last volume of the *Native Races* had been issued, Bancroft was in no hurry to begin publication of the *History of the
Pacific States*, the twenty-eight volume section which forms the
heart of the *Works*. He intended to issue the history with the imprint of A. L. Bancroft and Company, as the reception of the *Native
Races* had made the name of an eastern publisher unnecssary to help
sales.[20] However, he could not begin publication before 1879, the
year of expiration of the Appleton contract, without competing for
subscribers with Appleton's edition of the *Native Races*. Furthermore, Bancroft wanted to republish the earlier set so that it might be
sold with the history, as the first five volumes of the *Works* of Hubert Howe Bancroft.

As there was no pressure to put manuscript into print, Bancroft
did not immediately push ahead with plans for the completion of the
first volumes, although he determined the design of the work as a

[18] (New York: Appleton, 1875), 4. The *Native Races* was reissued by A. L.
Bancroft and Company in 1882, and the History Company in 1886. Many of the
same electrotype plates were used for all editions; several illustrations in the History
Company edition show signs of wear.

[19] Ephraim George Squier, *Nicaragua; its People, Scenery, Monuments and the
Proposed Interoceanic Canal* (New York: Appleton, 1856), 2 v., and *The Serpent
Symbol* (New York: Putnam, 1851), 254 pp., also John L. Stephens, *Incidents of
Travel in Central America* (New York: Harper, 1841), 2 v., and *Incidents of
Travel in Yucatan* (New York: Harper, 1843), 2 v. contain cuts which Bancroft
used in *Native Races* IV.

[20] Bancroft, *Literary Industries*, 586.

whole. He planned to divide his territory into regional sections and to write a separate history for each region, beginning with Central America.

Central America I was completed in 1881, and on October 10 of that year, typesetting was begun.[21] The book was published one year later, and a subsequent volume of the *Works* was issued every four months from October, 1882, to October, 1890.

The paper for the volumes was purchased in the East, but all work on the history—composing, electrotyping, printing, and binding—was done on the premises between 1882 and 1886. The same style and size of type were used for the newly issued volumes as for the *Native Races*, and when Bancroft reprinted the latter in 1883 he used the original plates except for half-title, title page, and dedication. The dedication page in *Native Races* I disappeared, and the title page now was headed: THE WORKS OF HUBERT HOWE BANCROFT. VOLUME I. THE NATIVE RACES.

The volumes making up the *History of the Pacific States* were numbered from south to north, beginning with *Central America* I–III, *Works* VI–VIII, and concluding with *Alaska, Works* XXXIII. The volumes which Bancroft called supplementary, *California Pastoral, California Inter Pocula, Popular Tribunals* (two volumes), *Essays and Miscellany*, and *Literary Industries*, were numbered as *Works* XXXIV–XXXIX.

They were not published in numerical order (table 1). When the assistants in the workshop began to set printed and manuscript sources in order, they found much more material indexed and ready for use on California than on Central America and Mexico. Bancroft let Oak begin writing on California as soon as the librarian finished his chores on the *Native Races*. Oak finished *California* I and *California* II long before volumes XVIII and XIX of the *Works* were due to be published in numerical sequence, and much of the work on the Spanish-speaking countries remained to be done. In order to create a defensible sequence, volumes were issued according to a chronological plan, the order of issue corresponding roughly to the

[21] Ibid., 585.

TABLE 1
PUBLICATION ORDER OF BANCROFT'S WORKS

Short title	Works number	Date of publication
Native Races I–V	I–V	1874–1875
Central America I (1501–1530)	VI	1882 October
Mexico I (1516–1521)	IX	1883 January
Mexico II (1521–1600)	X	April
Central America II (1530–1800)	VII	July
Mexico III (1600–1803)	XI	October
North Mexican States I (1531–1800)	XV	1884 January
California I (1542–1800)	XVIII	April
Northwest Coast I (1543–1800)	XXVII	July
Northwest Coast II (1800–1846)	XXVIII	October
Mexico IV (1804–1824)	XII	1885 January
Mexico V (1824–1861)	XIII	April
California II (1801–1824)	XIX	July
California III (1825–1840)	XX	October
Alaska (1730–1885)	XXXIII	1886 January
California IV (1840–1845)	XXI	April
California V (1846–1848)	XXII	August
Oregon I (1834–1848)	XXIX	October
British Columbia (1792–1887)	XXXII	1887 January
Central America III (1801–1887)	VIII	April
Popular Tribunals I (1851)	XXXVI	July
Popular Tribunals II (1856)	XXXVII	October
Mexico VI (1861–1887)	XIV	1888 January
California Pastoral (1769–1848)	XXXIV	April
California Inter Pocula (1848–1856)	XXXV	July
California VI (1848–1859)	XXIII	October
Oregon II (1848–1888)	XXX	1889 January
Arizona and New Mexico	XVII	April
North Mexican States and Texas II (1801–1889)	XVI	July
Utah	XXVI	October
Nevada, Colorado, and Wyoming	XXV	1890 January
Washington, Idaho, and Montana	XXXI	April
California VII (1860–1890)	XXIV	July
Essays and Miscellany	XXXVIII	October
Literary Industries	XXXIX	November

order of events described in the volume.[22] The sequence is the clearest between October 1883 and July 1884, when a volume on eighteenth-century central Mexico (*Mexico* III) was followed by one on North Mexico in the same period (*North Mexican States* I), California to 1800 (*California* I), and the Pacific Northwest to 1800 (*Northwest Coast* I).

During the campaign that followed the publication of *Central America* I, canvassers attempted to argue that this order of publication was an advantage to subscribers, stating that patrons of the history would find it easy to follow the story of the entire Pacific area as it was unfolded in successive volumes.[23] Whether or not this was true, the sequence of issue was an advantage to agents.

The initial volumes on Central America and Mexico attracted interest, as anticipated, because of the comparisons with Prescott's *History of the Conquest of Mexico.* Although subsequent volumes on Mexico received less attention, canvassers in the coastal states could stir up new interest by assuring prospective customers that volumes of local interest would be published regularly. Bancroft accented this local appeal in his preface to *Northwest Coast* I:

> Obviously, events affecting the area as a whole, before its division into separate domains, belong to each of the separate states; so that the *History of the Northwest Coast* may properly be regarded as preliminary to and part of the *History of Oregon,* the *History of Washington, Idaho and Montana,* and the *History of British Columbia.*[24]

The volumes of the history concerning the southwestern states and the states in the Great Basin were not published until 1889 and 1890, but the areas received some attention in 1886 when stories of Americans moving across them to settle in California and Oregon were told in *California* V and *Oregon* I. Contemporary volumes on all areas appeared late; those for areas in the United States except Alaska, for example, were not published until 1889 or 1890, and agents

---

[22] Ibid., 589. Henry Oak claims credit for the idea: Oak, *"Literary Industries" in New Light,* 61–62.

[23] Oak, *"Literary Industries" in a New Light,* 61–62.

[24] *Works* XXVII (San Francisco: A. L. Bancroft, 1884), vi.

canvassing as late as 1888 could pledge subscribers that Bancroft would use the dictations sent to him in the preparation of those volumes.

Canvassers for the *Works* were responsible to a division in the company devoted solely to selling the history. Two years before *Central America* I was published, Bancroft took the canvassing for the *Native Races* out of the hands of Theodore C. Smith, head of A. L. Bancroft and Company's subscription department, and set up the Bancroft's Works department to handle the campaign for the *Works*. To head the new department, he appointed Nathan Stone, a hard-working, ambitious New Englander, who had been a successful publisher in Japan.[25] Stone soon had an army of canvassers in the field.

Stone's manual for agents seems to have been quite similar to the manual used for the *Native Races*.[26] A speech was given for the agent to memorize as before, and instructions on manipulating the prospectus were included.

The form of the Bancroft prospectus was traditional, containing samples inside the front cover showing the appearance of the spine of a volume in various bindings. In a Bancroft prospectus issued in 1882, textual matter begins with thirteen pages of promotional material, describing successively the author, the library, and the work. A list of titles of all volumes and an "Introduction to the *History of the Pacific States*" is included. This is followed by extracts from the preface to *Central America* I, Bancroft's opinions of Prescott and Irving as historians, some mention of his assistants, and claims for the *History*. A map of Central America precedes forty sample pages gleaned from the entire volume.[27]

Title pages for *Central America* I and for *Mexico* I appear at various places in the prospectus. There are two of these pages for each

---

[25] Bancroft, *Literary Industries*, 586, 790, 793–794.

[26] [Nathan J. Stone], *Information for Agents to Assist in Selling the Works of Hubert H. Bancroft* (n.p., n.d.), quoted in: Caughey, 287–290. This booklet is not in Bancroft Library, and I have not seen a copy of it.

[27] All material from: *Prospectus of the Literary Works of Hubert Howe Bancroft* (San Francisco: A. L. Bancroft, 1882), 1 v.

book; one identifying the work as a volume in the *History of the Pacific States*, the other, as a volume in Bancroft's *Works*. Salesmen's weekly report forms have spaces for recording orders taken for the *History* and for the *Works*, as well as a third alternative, "Complete *Works* except *Native Races*."[28] The arrangement of the prospectus enabled the agent to talk his man up from a subscription for the twenty-eight volume *History* to one for the *Works*.

After going through the prospectus, the agent was expected to make use of pamphlets which contained all the compliments which had been showered on the *Native Races*. *What the World Says About It*, a sheet or two of brief laudatory quotations preceding the accounts of the content of the volumes was considered an impressive aid in making sales. The *Times*, the *North American Review*, the *Paris Review*, and other periodicals and newspapers of prestige carried something of the flavor of a good list of subscribers, and, by means of excerpts in this pamphlet the influence of their words was extended far beyond their readership. Other pamphlets were often made up of quoted commendations from literary and scientific men. Pamphlets were changed and reissued as the history progressed, and new reviews could be utilized. The department copied and recopied their best endorsements for years, however, like a canvasser copying a few good names on a fresh subscription list.

As important as pamphlets were, subscription lists were given their usual prominence, and the agent was urged to read and display his list of prominent subscribers. Bancroft's well-known customers, in agreeing to purchase the *Works*, were requested to sign a contract which constituted an endorsement. Bancroft had the subscription list placed on a blank with the following paragraph engraved at the top:

San Francisco, Cal.   188

To Hubert Howe Bancroft,
  Dear Sir:
    In token of our high appreciation of the value to the Pacific Coast, and to the world, of your long and arduous historical labors, in a new field and after a manner peculiar to yourself, we herewith tender our several sub-

[28] Forms among: [History Company Records].

scriptions to complete sets of your literary works in thirty-nine volumes, in number and style of binding as designated below, payments to be made at the regular published prices as the volumes are issued and delivered.[29]

The legend at the top of the form implicitly carries on the argument for patronage on the basis of the general importance of Bancroft's work which began with the *Native Races* canvass.

Surviving lists occasionally carry only one signature each; William T. Coleman signed an order for "twenty-five full sets, certain & probably fifty sets," and J. Rufino Barrios ordered one hundred sets, "75 cloth binding, 25 sheep." In San Francisco, where the Vigilantes of 1856 were remembered, Coleman's signature over such an order would serve the same purpose as a list. In Latin America the name of Barrios, president of Guatemala, would be equally impressive.

The engraved form was also used in Texas and other interior states, where the wording of the first phrase was changed to: "In token of my high appreciation of the value to the West and South. . . ." A specimen filled out in Fort Worth contains thirty-one signatures in two columns. The list is headed by the mayor and several attorneys. Further down are merchants, real estate agents, a pastor, and, near the bottom, a bookseller.

The request for information assumed greater importance in the canvass for the *Works* than it had in the earlier campaign for the *Native Races*. Bancroft expanded an idea of Mrs. Victor's to dimensions the lady had not foreseen. She complained about the matter to Judge Deady:

> As far as I could, I made note of each immigration [to Oregon] as it came, giving names. I had done this down to 1852, but after '48 they were cut out for want of room—and then Mr. Bancroft decided to *add* at the end of each vol. in the manner you complain of, everybody who *subscribes!* It is poor taste, but he thinks it necessary to financial success. The plan I followed was to include *everybody* in the immigrations and whoever made himself notable afterwards was duly mentioned in the place where he did something to signalize himself. . . .[30]

[29] Copies of all engraved forms in [History Company Records].
[30] Victor to Deady, June 18, 1883. Oregon Historical Society.

Canvassers asked for information concerning the lives and careers of the people whom they approached and took down anything that was volunteered. Many dictations secured from these interviews are very slight, limited to data on the subject's immediate family, his occupation, and the date and manner of his arrival in the West. Agents recorded the biographies in such a casual manner—on hotel stationery, blank book stock, and unidentifiable scraps—that Bancroft was moved to caution Nemos: "All letters containing information; and particularly all agents' reports on men and dictations, or brief notes, should be regarded—preserved and used. We have pledged our faith to do so."[31]

The dictations of subscribers *were* used. Seven volumes of the *Works—North Mexican States and Texas* II; *Arizona and New Mexico*; *California* VII; *Nevada, Colorado, and Wyoming*; *Utah*; *Oregon* II; and *Washington, Idaho, and Montana*—contain, among their footnotes, page upon page of biographical paragraphs concerning men of little historical significance. The paragraphs detract from the scholarly appearance of the histories, but they helped to sell books. A check of the one hundred and eighty-two dictations which were taken by agents in Arapahoe County, Colorado, shows that sixty-seven appear in notes for the Colorado chapters of *Nevada, Colorado, and Wyoming*. Fifty-five of these notes were taken from subscribers, according to information on the original dictations. Only two subscribers were left out, but one hundred and thirteen nonsubscribers were ignored.[32]

Another example of the use of subscribers' dictations may be found by comparing the work of two agents in Utah. Over one hundred and seventy dictations were taken by L. H. Nichols. The absence of account numbers or statement of subscription on these dictations indicates that none were given by subscribers, and none of the names appear in the *Utah* volume. Fifteen dictations taken in Utah by L. Leadbetter have been preserved. Eight bear account numbers, and seven of these subjects have one- or two-sentence bio-

[31] Bancroft to Nemos, November 26, 1884, no. 21.
[32] "Colorado Dictations: Arapahoe County." Bancroft Library.

graphical notices in appropriately placed footnotes in *Utah*.[33] Three others receive similar notice. This understanding between subscriber and agent was suspected by the Salt Lake *Tribune*, which accused Bancroft of daubing "historic whitewash" on selected saints for a fee,[34] but the record shows that the company was unintimidated. The agreements of agents were honored, and subscribers found a place in the work.[35]

The subscriber, whether he was attracted by the call to support the *Works* for the glory of the West, by the prospect of appearing in the history, or by a canvasser's appeals to his sense of parental duty, signed a contract agreeing to take four volumes a year at $4.50 or more per volume. A. L. Bancroft and Company fixed the price on their edition of the *Native Races* at the same minimum figure that they asked for the *History of the Pacific States*, one dollar less than Appleton had asked. The cost of the volumes, of course, increased as bindings became more showy.

The cheapest binding was maroon cloth with title (*Works* or *History of the Pacific States*), author, volume number, and title of volume, stamped in gold on the spine. The covers of the cloth volume were blind-stamped with a rule border and simple ornaments in the corners and center. For $5.50, the subscriber could have sheepskin with title and author stamped in gold on two black panels placed between the raised "cords"[36] on the spine. Half calf, half Russia, and

---

[33] See: "Utah Dictations." Bancroft Library, and *History of Utah* (San Francisco: History Co., 1889), 700, 704, 733.

[34] "Historic Whitewash, When and How it is to be Daubed on," Salt Lake City *Tribune*, December 24, 1884.

[35] *Central America* III, *Mexico* VI, and *British Columbia* are current volumes which are free from the subscriber biographies. N. W. Peake, writing from Mexico City, requested revisions in *Central America* III to accommodate biographies which he had promised subscribers, but the men whom he names do not appear in the book. —Peake to Savage, June 9, 1887, [History Company Records]. Bancroft wrote Nemos that he might close *Mexico* VI without biographical material, "as the subscriptions there do not amount to anything." —Bancroft to Nemos, [n.d.] no. 43b. British Columbia subscribers may be among the "authorities" whom Bancroft grouped near the end of his history of the province.

[36] All leather bindings have the ridges across the spine characteristic of many hand-bound books, but examination of bindings that have broken at the hinge

half morocco bindings sold for $8.00, and full morocco, full calf, or full Russia leather for $10.00. The more expensive bindings were generously gilt. The calf volumes had gold-stamped rules liberally distributed on the spine, a triple rule frame in gold on the covers, and arabesques and fleurons along top, bottom, and fore-edge extending inward to meet the end-papers, which were marbled to match the page edges.

Such opulence cost the subscriber to the *Works* $390 for the complete set, but the total cost of the thirty-nine volumes in any binding was never mentioned. Even the $175.50 charged for cloth was a formidable sum, and it was much easier to get the name on the dotted line by stressing the price per volume.

The successful agent received a commission ranging from $25.00 to $75.00 on each order,[37] the amount presumably depending on the binding selected by the subscriber. The return to the agent is small compared to the total cost of the set, but a canvasser would earn as much with one sale of the *Works* in cloth binding as a literary assistant received for a work week of sixty hours.

Whether the agent succeeded in taking an order or not, he was to turn in a report of each interview. The company printed at the head of its form "Agent's Report on Persons Seen," exactly what information was wanted:

> The Agent will make a full report about every person whom he calls to subscribe, whether that person subscribes or not. State name, address, occupation, standing in the community, pecuniary responsibility and the result of the solicitation. If the person subscribes, state to what he subscribes. If he does not subscribe at all, state what he says about it, and how will be the best way to approach him in the future.[38]

---

shows no trace of cords at the ridges. There are three equally spaced recessed cords instead.

[37] *Stone v. Bancroft*, Transcript on Appeal, Superior Court, City and County of San Francisco (1895), 164. Testimony of H. H. Bancroft: "The property... consisted in...some seven thousand and two or three hundred orders for the histories which had been taken at a cost of from $25 to $75 an order...."

[38] "The Works of Hubert Howe Bancroft; Agent's Report on Persons Seen," single sheets in [History Company Records].

This, of course, was a purely business report, separate from the dictation. The dictation went to the library; the report remained in the Bancroft's Works department.

No reports are available from the most successful canvassers: George H. Morrison, who rose to a position of great trust in the Bancroft office after a term of canvassing in Nevada; Professor Edwin W. Fowler, who secured subscriptions from George Hearst, William Sharon, Claus Spreckels, Adolph Sutro, and other men of equal prominence; or from Colonel L. S. Hatch, who in April 1886, with a quota of two sales per day, was "at the head of the list,"[39] among all Bancroft's canvassers. Only these report forms submitted after unsuccessful canvasses were preserved, as they were needed by the department to direct promotional correspondence. They give a vivid picture of the day-to-day grind of the ordinary canvasser:[40]

J. E. Durham is a close fellow and thinks the work entirely to [*sic*] high. He is one of those fellows who thinks a book agent is a public robber.

W. H. Reardon, College City, Colusa County, Cal.
School teacher being prominent having taught school for the last 10 years and having a great deal of real estate but not of literary turn of mind. Has Native races and wishes to dispose of them. He would like the history but wants to exchange these 5 volumes for 5 of the History and not be compelled to receive the races again. [*sic*].

Morison Bryan, Orland, Collusa [*sic*] Cal.
Quite well to do. Single gentleman. Pioneer. Has a good memory of old times. Would like the work but could not make up his mind as he thinks more of the coin than he does of any reading. Estimated wealth sixty thousand dollars. Farmer. Has considerable influence and think that writing him would be a waste of time for I have now wasted 7½ hours with him.

The reports show clearly that for many agents the work was hard and rebuffs were frequent. Some agents had poor qualifications; they were poorly educated and must have had difficulty in winning the

---

[39] Hatch to N. J. Stone, April 24, 1886. In "Colorado Dictations, Arapahoe County," Bancroft Library.
[40] Reports quoted from: H. C. Osmurt, n.p., n.d.; F. A. Gilley, August 2, 1886; F. A. Gilley, August 27, 1886, [History Company Records].

confidence of their auditors. Others had poor territories; like Nichols in Utah, they had to try to sell the *Works* in areas which had been previously canvassed. Unable to win the commissions which had attracted them to the profession, a few canvassers were tempted to make their work easier by deceiving prospective patrons.

The company was frequently beset by claims of fraud from patrons since agents made unauthorized promises which they did not communicate to the department. Occasionally, canvassers misled subscribers as to the number of volumes in the *Works*. In one instance resulting in a suit, a prospect, mesmerized by the canvasser's spate of words, discovered that he had signed a contract for thirty-nine volumes while under the impression that he was ordering only one volume, a work which would contain his own biography. The court ruled that, as he could read, he should have read what he was signing, and granted him no remedy.[41]

As prominent a businessman as Leland Stanford could be equally careless. In 1890 he alleged to a Bancroft agent that he had been asked years before to support a projected history of California in five or six volumes. Accepting this representation without question, he had given his subscription to forty copies of the *Works*. Instead of six volumes, there were thirty or forty, and he had a storeroom filled with them. He felt the project had been misrepresented to him, and he would accept no more volumes.[42] As there could have been only three or four more volumes to be issued when Stanford took this stand, Bancroft did not attempt to take the matter to court.

A general rebellion of subscribers occurred in Montana,[43] which apparently had been hastily and carelessly canvassed. Bancroft's first concern was not to defend his history, but to get a few facts about his canvassers. In a letter to an aide he wrote:

[41] "History Company v. Daugherty," *Pacific Reporter*, XXIX (1892), 649–652.

[42] George T. Clark, "Leland Stanford and H. H. Bancroft's 'History'; a Bibliographical Curiosity," *Papers of the Bibliographical Society of America*, XXVII (1933), 20–21.

[43] This unrest lasted according to newspaper articles and correspondence from 1884 to 1886. Newspaper articles appeared in the Helena *Independent*, October 14, 1885, and February 25, 1886, and the Bozeman *Weekly Avant Courier*, May 13, 1886.

I wish you could find out what promises had been made by the canvassers about putting people in the book, and if they took the information necessary to fulfill the promise made. And have I got the stuff in the Library....

We certainly do not want to allow ourselves to be placed in a false position by our agents, and then have a great howl raised in 2 or 3 years.... It all comes from the agent's being too lazy to write out what he has promised and not caring for us or the work or the people or the subscribers or country further than to get their money out of it. We are not on it, [sic] and Stone is going to stop every man if he can't make the canvass without fooling people.[44]

Subscriptions obtained without deception often turned "bad." The cost of the volumes, $18 to $40 a year, was high, and, over the eight-year period during which the volumes were issued, subscribers' circumstances might change Patrons subscribing after 1882 also had to agree to pay in installments for volumes already issued, and many regretted their decisions after the canvasser had left. As agents were not required to deliver their orders, a responsibility that would soon have taken all of a reasonably good canvasser's time, the department could not take advantage of the brusque and intimidating demeanor used by canvassers in delivering other works. If a package sent by express or post were refused, the matter had to be handled by cajolery or court action, and the outcome of either was uncertain.

Problems in the field were aggravated by one which had its roots in the office. Stone, Bancroft, and Nemos pressed the campaign within the company, so that employees felt obliged to subscribe for the *Works* in order to hold their positions.[45] Even at a 50 percent discount from the regular subscriber's price,[46] the history was not wanted by many of the staff and was immediately sold for what it

---

[44] Bancroft to R. D. Faulkner, November 26, 1884, [History Company Records].

[45] Oak, *"Literary Industries" in a New Light*, 13; also note in William Nemos hand on receipt for cash paid for *Works*: "I as chief set an example to others on the staff not to expect free gift of Bancroft's history but to subscribe," no. 50; and *Public Opinion* (San Francisco), May 19, 1883.

[46] Nemos' receipt (Nemos' letter no. 50) is written for: "Fifty-four and 00/100 (27^{00} cash, 27^{00} discount) on account of Bancroft's Works in full of all demands." From his comment quoted in the previous note, it is reasonable to assume that the discount was not a privilege extended only to him.

would bring. As a consequence, from July 1885 to the end of the
campaign, Samuel Carson and Company and King Brothers, two
San Francisco bookselling firms, were offering volumes of the *Works*
at half price as soon as they were issued.[47] This unforeseen development must have hurt canvassers working in San Francisco, but Bancroft and Stone continued to press the canvass in other areas.

The orders which brought problems left the clearest traces; the
successful agent and the contented subscriber did not excite attention. Many errors were made, but most orders taken were made
good. The usual order form was not the fancy script tribute as signed
by Coleman and Barrios, but a brief contract form, clearly stating
the number of volumes subscribed for, the style of binding, and the
price of each volume.[48] Before May 1886 canvassers had returned
over seven thousand[49] of them to the department, properly signed for
subscriptions to the *History* or the *Works*.

[47] *Publishers' Weekly*, XXVIII (July 25 and August 1, 1885), 144, 176, for first
Carson advertisements. Ibid., XXIX (January 2, 1886), for first King Brothers
advertisement. Carson advertisements every week or so to 1889; King Brothers
to 1891.
[48] Sample form in: "Scrapbook of Materials about Hubert Howe Bancroft, his
Works, and the Bancroft Library." Bancroft Library.
[49] *Stone v. Bancroft*, 164, 201. Testimony of H. H. Bancroft.

CHAPTER VI

THE AUTHOR AS AGENT

SEVEN THOUSAND subscriptions was the original target for western sales of the *Native Races* alone.[1] Bancroft stated that three editions of one thousand each, of the five-volume set were printed and bound by the Riverside Press, "being followed by other thousands."[2] It is doubtful whether printing and sale exceeded three thousand by any sizeable margin, because the author would have taken pleasure in recording a popular success as much as he enjoyed recording his critical triumphs.

Despite the record of prices charged for printing, binding, and paper by the Riverside Press, a partial summary of composition costs in Bancroft's hand, and his record of his agreement with Appleton,[3] the lack of data concerning sales makes it impossible to gauge his total returns on the *Native Races*. Two factors, the cost of the cuts used in *Native Races* IV and the return to Bancroft as Pacific Coast agent for Appleton in selling the work, are also unknown.

Those figures which are given, however, show that all returns to

[1] [*Confidential*], 4, "Scrapbook of Materials about Hubert Howe Bancroft, His Works, and the Bancroft Library."

[2] Bancroft, *Literary Industries*, 336.

[3] Bancroft, "Composition Costs and Printing Information Concerning the *Native Races*," 1–3, [History Company Records] Bancroft, "Personal Observations during a Tour through the Line of Missions in Upper California," 193; Bancroft, *Literary Industries*, 346.

Bancroft on the first printing would probably be required to cover the cost of composition as well as printing and binding. Production profits would start with the second edition. Although the percentage of Bancroft's agency commission and the number of each style of binding sold are unknown variables, profits would probably run slightly over $10,000 for each thousand sets sold.[4] It is clear that a total sale of three or four thousand sets would realize less than half of $70,000, the figure given as the cost of the set.[5]

Bancroft was disappointed in Appleton's failure to make an aggressive attempt to sell the set[6] and also probably disappointed in A. L. Bancroft and Company's subscription department. Although he placed the sale of the history under Nathan Stone in a separate division of the company, he remained solicitous—very much aware of sales and concerned with contacts that might win or retain customers.

This change in attitude after the sale of the history began is evident in Bancroft's journals and correspondence, and in the publicity (or

[4] Bancroft's figures on composition do not include volume V and are, as he wrote, probably erroneous for volume II, which is listed at slightly more than half the figure for volumes I and III. The, first three *Native Races* volumes present the same problems to the compositor. Volume IV, because of its many illustrations, has much less text than the others. Volume V has a one-hundred-page index, set in double columns, which might have made it more costly. Totals for the volumes are: I, $1,700; II, $899; III, $1,817; IV, $816.

As author, Bancroft netted half of Appleton's retail price less the cost of printing and binding. For cloth, this amounted to $2.75 less $.90, or $1.85 per volume. For sheepskin, he received $3.25 less $1.35, or $1.90 per volume. (Figures and sources given in Chapter IV above.) A complete edition of 5,000 copies in cloth would bring him $9,250, and the same number of copies in leather would return $9,500 for his share as author. His share as agent was large enough so that he could cut the price of the sheepskin edition from $6.50 to $6.00 per volume within his territory, which included the Pacific Coast and the Great Basin. He did not set down his reasons for making this reduction, but he may have wanted to attract subscribers to the sheep binding, expecting them to buy the *History of the Pacific States* in a matching binding.

[5] "Why the Public should avail themselves of the earliest possible opportunity to secure the great Pacific Coast Work, 'The Native Races of the Pacific States'...." In "Notices and Reviews of the Library and of the 'Native Races of the Pacific States'."

[6] Bancroft, *Literary Industries*, 347.

lack of publicity) which attended his travels in search of information for use in his work. With the notable exception of his trip to the East on behalf of the *Native Races* in 1874, his major journeys in the 1870s were not concerned with gathering reviews or stimulating sales. He interrupted his wedding trip in 1876 for interviews with the Frémonts as well as for the Sutter dictation,[7] out of a desire to make his history as full and as fair as possible. A tour of southern California in 1874 and of the Pacific Northwest in 1878 were undertaken purely to gather data. On each of the latter trips, Bancroft knew well in advance what he wanted to see and where to find it.

Accompanied by his daughter, Kate, and Henry Oak, Bancroft sailed for San Diego in February 1874. He kept a journal during the tour of the California missions which began in San Diego, setting down his purpose on the first page:

> This I intend to be the first of a series of literary excursions, in which I hope to obtain not only much information from the archives lodged in various corners, and from living witnesses of historical scenes but a better knowledge of the countries in which those scenes were acted and of the people who took part in them.[8]

His account of his subsequent experience displays the same singleness of purpose. His major triumph during the journey was the acquisition of the collection of 129 scrapbooks of Californiana accumulated between 1850 and 1874 by Judge Benjamin Hayes. When Bancroft arrived in San Diego on February 21, he called upon the judge at once.[9] Two days later the historian persuaded Hayes to sell them the collection. Bancroft was elated as he deemed the collection "by far the most important in the state outside my own."[10] Other rewards of the journey were less spectacular, although Bancroft, with Judge Hayes' help, was able to start his program of having mission records copied for the library.[11]

[7] Ibid., 460.
[8] Bancroft, "Personal Observations....," 1.
[9] Ibid., 8. (Number of scrapbooks given in *California*, I, liv.)
[10] Ibid., 23, 25.
[11] Bancroft, *Literary Industries*, 513–523.

From May to July of 1878 Bancroft and his wife traveled through the Pacific Northwest, sailing to Victoria for a month's stay and returning by land through Washington and Oregon. Once more the historian clearly set down his aims:

> To examine public archives and private papers, to extract such portions as were useful in my work, to record and carry back with me the experiences of those who had taken an active part in the discovery and occupation of the country—these, together with a desire to become historically inspired with the spirit of settlement throughout the great north-west, [*sic*] constituted the burden of my mission.[12]

Although written in the full-blown style Bancroft favored in his published writings, the statement is essentially the same as the one found in the journal quoted earlier. The historian's description of his activities is similar also. He arranged for the copying of archives, wooed manuscript records from other leading collectors—A. C. Anderson of Victoria and Elwood Evans of Olympia, in this case— and took valuable dictations from Oregon pioneers. He wanted to meet Frances Fuller Victor, at this time an independent and well-known writer, but she was in southern Oregon gathering material. Bancroft wrote from San Francisco after his return and persuaded her to join his staff.[13]

In *Literary Industries*, Bancroft gave the names of over forty persons who lent him aid during this journey, as well as detailing the records that he found. His statements appear to be simple, though full, expressions of gratitude for aid received and reassertions of his authorities rather than the *quid pro quo* notices accorded to subscribers in the body and notes of the history. Bancroft's stay in Victoria was noted twice in the local press, and his progress through Oregon is mentioned in four local papers with an appeal for information for the history. These articles did, of course, publicize the *History of the Pacific States*, as did similar notices in San Francisco and Sacramento newspapers.[14] All articles, moreover, assisted Bancroft in his primary

---

[12] Ibid., 531.

[13] Ibid., 530–551.

[14] Bancroft's visit in British Columbia was noted by the Victoria *Colonist* on May 7, and the Victoria *Standard* on May 29. Notices appeared in the following

purpose, gathering material for the history of the Northwest. In the years following his return, *Northwest Coast* I and II and *British Columbia* were written.

The publication of the history caused an increasing shift in emphasis in Bancroft's later journeys. Although he wanted to become acquainted with the country and its people on his trip to Mexico in the fall and winter of 1883–1884, he was also interested in having Mexico become acquainted with him. Two volumes of Mexican history had been issued and a third was due in October 1883. The *Native Races* experience had taught the historian that his work required aggressive salesmanship to succeed. Therefore, he was eager to have himself and his work presented in the Mexican press. The journalists of Mexico receive more attention in his notes on the trip than any other public figures except General Porfirio Díaz.

Bancroft was again accompanied by his daughter, Kate, now twenty-three, and by A. C. Cabezut, a secretary and interpreter.[15] Before they reached Monterey, the journey assumed a distinctly different color from the preceding ones. Bancroft wrote Stone about it:

> Monterey, Mex.   Sept. 11th 1883
>
> Dear Stone:
>
> Cabezut has managed to pick up eleven orders so far, as we came along, several of them on the cars. Mexico and Spanish America are just as good fields as any other to a certain extent. Of course there is not as much in them, for the language is different, and the people are very poor and very illiterate. The upper classes have not much to boast of in way of learning and accomplishments, but some copies can be placed all over Spanish America with certainty, by a competent person.
>
> Of course what we do in this way does not amount to anything so far as thorough work is concerned. It would take from 3 to 5 years to go

---

Oregon papers: *New Northwest* (Portland), June 21, *Willamette Farmer* (Salem), June 21, Jacksonville *Democrat Times*, July 5, and Ashland *Tidings*, July 5. The Sacramento *Record Union*, July 8 (?), reprinted in San Francisco *Bulletin*, July 9, and San Francisco *Call*, July 9, printed notices of the Bancrofts' return. (All dates, 1878).

[15] Hubert Howe Bancroft, "Notes on Mexico in 1883" (handwritten), 4. Bancroft Library.

over the 27 states of Mexico with any degree of thoroughness.

As we approach the city of Mexico I shall stop all soliciting orders, as we do not want to enter the capital in the guise of canvassers.

With best respects

H H Bancroft

In fact the field for selling this book is the world over. Some parts of it of course are better than others, but the firm of A.L.B. & Co. will make the greatest mistake of their lives if they don't continue this work all over the world as time and opportunity offer to do it profitably.[16]

Bancroft did not neglect to inspect libraries along his route. He thought those in Monterey and Saltillo of little worth, but the San Luis Potosí state library he found admirable. In Mexico City he visited the national library and secured permission to copy much material from the national archives.[17] He searched in the archives and in other places for material to send Nemos, whom he had asked to become an authority on nineteenth-century Mexico.[18] At the end of his stay, the historian had a trunk and eleven cases of books to return to the library.[19]

There was nothing hasty or superficial, therefore, about Bancroft's investigations. He was limited by his lack of facility in Spanish in communicating with the Mexicans, but he did persuade General Díaz to dictate his memoirs for a biography which Bancroft expected to be "*the* book of the day in Mexico."[20] General Díaz, who was president-elect of Mexico at the time, dictated to the historian from 2 P.M. to 6 P.M. each day during December 1883.[21]

In his letters to Nemos and in his entries concerning the Díaz biography in his notes, Bancroft made it clear that he anticipated a great popular sale for the biography, which was to be published in English and Spanish editions.[22] He probably also looked forward to

---

[16] Bancroft to Stone, September 11, 1883, [History Company Records].

[17] Bancroft, *Literary Industries*, 701–703, 741.

[18] Bancroft to Nemos, October 30, 1883, no. 19, and December 22, 1883, no. 36.

[19] Bancroft, "Notes on Mexico in 1883," 208.

[20] Bancroft to Nemos, October 30, 1883, no. 19.

[21] Bancroft, "Notes on Mexico in 1883," 207.

[22] Bancroft to Nemos, December 26, 1883, no. 3b.

an increased demand for his history after the biography was published.

However, even before his introduction to Díaz he had met Ygnacio M. Altamirano and Alfredo Chavero, leading journalists of Mexico City, who delighted the Californian by professing great interest in the history and offering to review it. Before either of them did so, the editor of *La Patria*, a weekly newspaper, published Bancroft's picture and gave his volumes several reviews.[23] Bancroft also received support from Vicente García Torres, editor and proprietor of *El Monitor Republicano*, "the only really first-class independent paper in Mexico," who gave the historian two or three flattering notices and helped him gather material. Bancroft found García Torres most sympathetic, "altogether the most Yankeefied Mexican in the journalistic fraternity."[24]

Before Bancroft left Mexico, he received a hard lesson. He had given sets of his books to Altamirano, Chavero, and to Vicente Riva Palacio, a gentleman who had impressed him at their first meeting as one of the finest men in America, excelling all Americans and Europeans in courtesy. After two months had passed, without the promised notices from the three writers, the historian was forced to admit: "I think I smell a rat. . . ." He expanded this statement in the following passage:

All promised everything, Mexican-like, and Mexican-like, did nothing. I attributed to [*sic*] the national infirmity at first, but lately I have my suspicions that a conspiracy is afoot. Two of the men are interested in the work commissioned to be done by the government; history of Mexico work I mean. They can hope to do no such work as mine unless indeed they use my books, because they cannot put the necessary labor on it. In proportion as they praise my book the less the necessity for theirs will appear. I judge this from the fact that the excuses for not making the promised review by all three, which were exceedingly bland at first are now delivered to me in a shorter style, always polite even now but evidently not honest. They do not exactly want to condemn; they will not praise.[25]

[23] Bancroft, "Notes on Mexico in 1883," 71.
[24] Ibid., 72.
[25] Ibid., 187–188.

Bancroft swallowed his frustration as he became absorbed with the Díaz biography. Cabezut had taken one hundred orders for the history in Mexico, and was now engaged to translate for the historian. Two Mexican stenographers took down the general's words, working on alternate days.[26] Bancroft relayed his plans to Nemos:

> Gen Diaz dictates to me now every day 4 hours which is good work for a Mexican. Much of it will go almost bodily into the biog. It will require rewriting, of course, but if that which is to go with it is well arranged and in good shape it will be impossible for anyone to write it up at so slow a pace as 4 or 5 pages a day.
>
> You might be thinking who in San Francisco will put it into the purest & best Spanish and what he will do the job for, say 700 pages, all coarse type, say 50 pages of illustration to come out leaving 650.[27]

On January 10, Bancroft left Mexico, stopping at Austin, Texas, to observe the state legislature in session on his way back to California.[28] Despite the amount of material collected for the history, his journey had been quite different from his earlier tours. He had encouraged his assistant to canvass as soon as they entered Mexico, and his letters to Stone and to Nemos show that he looked on the country as a market for the history, as well as a source of historical material. His contacts with the Mexican press demonstrated a self-confidence very different from the nervousness and uncertainty which he had felt before canvassing New England. Although he did not receive the notices he sought, he was certain that the lack of response of the Mexican journalists was an acknowledgment of the merit of his work, rather than a denial of its worth. Finally, in a unique departure from his role as Pacific States historian, Bancroft had spent afternoons for over a month in gathering material for what he hoped would be a popular biography to be sold separately from his *Works*.

The historian returned to San Francisco on March 17, 1884, after a brief vacation in Ojai, California. In August of the same year he

26 Ibid., 207.
27 Bancroft to Nemos, December 26, 1883, no. 3b.
28 "Notes on Mexico in 1883," 208–209.

went to Salt Lake City with his wife and son Philip for the sake of the boy's health. While in Utah the older Bancrofts interviewed pioneers and examined documents, Mrs. Bancroft's role being to get the woman's viewpoint—on polygamy among other questions.[29] One of the most important works that Bancroft had not seen before was a twenty-volume manuscript journal written by Mormon Apostle Wilford Woodruff, giving a detailed history of the church and its members from their settlement in Nauvoo.[30] Despite the new material, Bancroft's correspondence with Nemos indicated that most of the research on Utah had been done and that assistants Bates and Newkirk were at work on the manuscript of the *History of Utah*.[31] The historian's purpose in talking to numbers of Mormons was to add color to his history and to gain friends and potential subscribers.

In October Bancroft traveled to Denver, where he introduced general agent, Colonel L. S. Hatch. His letters to his assistant, Richard D. Faulkner, usually with regard to notices in the press, show that publicity and subscribers were uppermost in his mind at this time.[32]

He was still collecting data, however. In a letter to Nemos he urged its preservation:

> What I send from here & elsewhere I hope will be preserved. I go to no end of trouble and expense sometimes to get apparrently insignificant things. The MS, even the pencil sketches which are by way up men usually, and ought to be pasted on to scrap book paper & bound, should be bound and used.... [*sic*][33]

The "insignificant things" are undoubtedly dispersed through the collection of over fifty dictations and transcripts taken by Bancroft, his wife, and his daughter Kate, in Colorado.[34] He also wrote briefly

[29] Bancroft, *Literary Industries,* 759–761, also, M. G. Bancroft to Nemos, September 9, 1884, no. 41.

[30] Bancroft, *Literary Industries,* 761.

[31] Bancroft to Nemos, November 26, 1884, no. 21—passage quoted on p. 22 above.

[32] Bancroft to Faulkner, October 19, 22, November 12, 1884, [History Company Records].

[33] Bancroft to Nemos, November 26, 1884, no. 21.

of his own impressions of the citizens of the state on a few folios of lined foolscap. In these "Colorado Notes," he expressed gratitude to William N. Byers, editor of the *Rocky Mountain News*, and Wilbur F. Stone, a justice of the Colorado Supreme Court, saying: "I should take his [Byers'] and Judge Stone's dictations and make them the base of the history of Colorado and add to them (after I had formed the skeleton) from other sources."[35] Bancroft may have followed his proposal to found the Colorado history on the work of the two men, but there are nine hundred and thirty-seven dictations and other manuscripts garnered between 1885 and 1887 by his staff, in addition to the material accumulated by the historian and his family in 1884. Seven hundred or more of these are brief dictations submitted by agents.[36]

When Bancroft visited New Mexico and Texas, he already had the Spanish and French sources for the history of the region, and had planned to place Arizona and New Mexico together in a volume of the *History of the Pacific States*. The proposed volume is mentioned in the Preface to *North Mexican States* I, published in January 1884 a work which included fifty-three pages on the history of Texas during the seventeenth and eighteenth centuries.

In the 1884 edition, the subject of Texas is introduced in the following words:

It is my purpose as elsewhere explained to include in these volumes on a certain scale, the history of Texas down to the time when that country ceased to be a Spanish or Mexican province. Obviously the record could not be omitted from a *History of the North Mexican States*, however slight may seem to some the connection between a gulf coast province and the Pacific States. The peculiarity of territorial relations, however, justifies, as my limits of space necessitate, a more general treatment than is accorded to other parts of the country. Minor details must be omitted. . . .[37]

[34] Bancroft Library, *A Guide to the Manuscript Collections of the Bancroft Library*, edited by Dale L. Morgan and George P. Hammond (Berkeley: University of California Press, 1963), v. 1, 185–242, *passim*.
[35] Hubert Howe Bancroft, "Colorado Notes" (handwritten), 1884, 2. Bancroft Library.
[36] Bancroft Library, *Guide . . .*, 185–242.
[37] Hubert Howe Bancroft, *The History of the North Mexican States*, I, *Works*, XV (San Francisco: A. L. Bancroft, 1884), 379.

Shortly after these words were published Bancroft changed his mind and resolved to treat Texas more extensively. In the 1886 edition, the words *and Texas* were added to the title, and more details on the early history of the area were supplied in one hundred pages devoted to the state. The introductory passage reads:

> It is my purpose as elsewhere explained to include in these volumes the history of Texas down to the time when that country ceased to be a Mexican province, *after which period it will receive more general treatment.* Obviously the record could not be omitted from a *History of the North Mexican States,* however slight may seem to some the connection between a gulf coast province and the Pacific States. The peculiarity of territorial relations, *and the remarkable circumstances under which Texas acquired her independence of Mexico, justify the introduction of her history, and it would be classified as incomplete if all information about her subsequent career were suppressed.* Minor details however, of no importance have been avoided. . . .[38]

Bancroft decided to make Texas a "Pacific State" after his visit in Austin on his return from Mexico, and by January 1885 an agent was busy in Galveston.[39] In April 1885 *Mexico* V was published. The volume contains an account of the war between the United States and Mexico written, of course, as a part of Mexican history. Texas papers were generous in their reviews, but sales figures are unavailable. Texans may have needed an additional stimulus to bring them to subscribe for the *Works.*

In October 1885 the author set out on a personal appearance tour of the Southwest accompanied by agents, Colonels J. T. Grayson and George H. Morrison. Newspaper notices of their travels indicate that the trio did not have time for very serious research.

In Las Vegas, New Mexico, Colonel Grayson arranged a celebration for the historian, a banquet, whose guest list included about one hundred leading citizens of the state. After a ten-course dinner with

---

[38] Hubert Howe Bancroft, *The History of the North Mexican States and Texas,* I, *Works,* XV (San Francisco: History Company, 1886), 379. (Italics for emphasis mine.) This is not presented by the publisher as a revised edition. Some copies of 1884 edition include *and Texas* on title page.

[39] Galveston *Daily News,* January 24, 1885.

four wines, Grayson proposed several toasts, and Bancroft responded
to the first with "a very eloquent address."[40] Other toasts and
speeches followed, and the versatile Grayson brought the evening
to a close with a few songs. A local paper reported the historian's
reactions:

> Mr. Bancroft seemed highly pleased to meet so many representative
> New Mexico people gathered about him to do honor to his presence. He
> no doubt appreciates that men of this country are worthy of recognition,
> and, in his forthcoming works they will no doubt be kindly referred to.[41]

Bancroft's trip through Texas was as rapid as a political campaign
tour. On October 30 he arrived in El Paso with Grayson and visited
the office of the *Daily Times*. The editor immediately pronounced
them: "men of the right stripe and . . . pleasant people to meet anywhere."[42] Bancroft carried with him three-by-five-inch printed
cards stating his mission. They were apparently designed to save local
dignitaries the trouble of writing endorsements in their own words:

> Mr. Hubert H. Bancroft of California, who has spent a lifetime and a
> fortune in gathering the material for and writing a full and reliable history
> of the western half of North America, is now making an extended tour
> through Texas with the same purpose in view, the State of Texas being
> included in his work. Mr. Bancroft's object in this visit is to come per-
> sonally in contact with as many of the leading men in Texas as possible,
> and gather from them their ideas and experiences regarding the history
> of the country, its resources and general development, and any other
> information pertinent to his great work.
>
> As this most laborious undertaking is in every way highly beneficial to
> the material and intellectual interests of the State; and as both Mr. Ban-
> croft and his historical works are endorsed by the highest authorities in
> America and Europe, we bespeak for him a hearty welcome and efficient
> aid.[43]

Bancroft remained in El Paso two days. From November 4 to
November 6 he was in Fort Worth, and Dallas papers report his

---

40 Las Vegas *Gazette*, October 25, 1885.

41 *Daily Optic* (Las Vegas), October 26, 1885.

42 El Paso *Daily Times*, October 30, 1885.

43 Copy pasted in "Criticisms on H. H. Bancroft's Works. A collection of
Newspaper Clippings, 1878–1887" (Scrapbook). Bancroft Library.

A. L. Bancroft & Company Building. Courtesy Bancroft Library, University of California.

William Nemos. Courtesy Bancroft
Library, University of California.

Henry L. Oak. Courtesy Bancroft Library, University of California.

Frances Fuller Victor. Courtesy Oregon Historical Society.

The History Building. Courtesy Bancroft Library, University of California.

The Bancroft Library, Valencia Street, San Francisco. Courtesy Bancroft Library, University of California.

visit on November 8. He and Morrison were in Waco on November 11, and on November 12 the Waco paper reported that Bancroft was "heading south."[44] No further newspaper records of the journey are available, but south of Waco lie Austin and San Antonio—important cities then as now, and presumably the historian visited them. On November 26 Bancroft was at home at his ranch in Walnut Creek, California, complaining to Nemos of "a bad cold contracted on the cars."[45] There is no reference to material gathered during the journey in the letter.

Once A. L. Bancroft and Company had begun to publish the history, Bancroft could not resist attempting to increase sales by every method which occurred to him. Playing the role of celebrated author was only one of the many means at his command. His practice of including subscribers in the history has been mentioned. He also pushed the campaign by soliciting the help of prominent friends, by promising reciprocal favors for subscriptions, and by utilizing every means of communication with subscribers and prospective subscribers from personal letters to "news" articles.

One of the most cooperative of friends was Judge Matthew P. Deady, who had read and approved the *History of Oregon* in proof. In May 1883 L. Leadbetter, a canvasser, visited the judge in Portland with letters from Bancroft and Fred Stone, Nathan's brother, a Bancroft employee who had long corresponded with Deady concerning book orders. Bancroft asked Deady to look at all of the Oregon history in print, which Leadbetter carried with him, and show it to three or four other experts in Oregon history. After this was done, Bancroft continued, he would be grateful if Deady would write a "Certificate" of commendation, "that the people of Oregon may have some knowledge of what they are going to get as I approach their territory."[46] Bancroft closed his letter by offering to change anything that was not right.

[44] El Paso *Daily Times*, October 31, November 1; Fort Worth *Daily Mail*, November 4, Fort Worth *Daily Gazette*, November 6; Dallas *Daily Herald* and Dallas *Morning News* both November 8; Waco *Daily Examiner*, November 11, 12. (All dates 1885.)

[45] Bancroft to Nemos, November 26, 1885, no. 44b.

[46] Bancroft to Deady, May 15, 1883. Oregon Historical Society.

Stone's letter asked Deady to introduce Leadbetter to "forty or fifty of the best men of Portland," and also offered to exchange the cloth-bound volumes Deady had purchased for volumes bound in sheepskin. Deady would be given a refund on what he had paid and would receive the remainder of the *Works*, in sheep, free of charge.[47]

Deady gave the requested letters immediately but was slower to accept the proferred refund and offer of free volumes. On June 3 he wrote Bancroft saying that he was much pleased with what he had read, that it would be invaluable, and that the notes gave an eyewitness atmosphere. He then asked that Mrs. Deady's parents, Robert and Rhoda Henderson, be mentioned, gave biographical data concerning them, and stated: "I think they deserve a niche in your Pantheon of Oregon worthies, and 'we all' won't like it if they are not given one on pages 567 and 625 or elsewhere."[48] As often happened when Deady requested changes in material which was in page proof, Bancroft did not choose to alter the text although he could not ignore so pointed a request. The Hendersons appear "elsewhere," in a liberal footnote on page 144 of *Oregon* II.

In his letter of June 3, Deady had enclosed a postal order for $4.50 for volume V of the *History of the Pacific States*. Nathan Stone sent him a letter in September 1883 stating that it was Mr. Bancroft's wish that he should have the volumes free and in leather. A refund check was enclosed.[49] There is no further correspondence on the subject, and it may be assumed that Deady accepted the second offer.

If prospective subscribers were unimpressed with the endorsement of leading citizens, some of those who had business relations with A. L. Bancroft and Company might have been encouraged to subscribe by a letter which they received early in the campaign.

> 721 Market St.,
> San Francisco, ——— 188
>
> Dear Sir:
>
> By to-day's mail, we forward a few circulars, reviews & c. pertaining to the literary works of our Mr. H. H. Bancroft, who has devoted 20 years of study and over $500,000 upon this enterprise.

[47] F. P. Stone to Deady, May 16, 1883. Oregon Historical Society.

[48] Deady to Bancroft, June 3, 1883, in Deady, M. P. "Letters, dictations and related biographical material, 1874–1889." Bancroft Library.

[49] N. J. Stone to Deady, September 12, 1883. Oregon Historical Society.

The first vols. on Central America and Mexico are just out, and then new vols. will appear at the rate of 3 or 4 per annum, thereby making the payments easy.

We would be very much pleased to enter your name as a subscriber to this work ($4.50 every 4 months) which is one of the largest of its kind ever undertaken in the U.S., and one we hope will be supported and appreciated by the public.

If we are honored we would endeavor to reciprocate the favor during our business relationship, and will also esteem it highly.

Hoping to be favored by the order.

    We remain,
        Yours truly,
Note: One Vol. every 4 months.[50]

Henry Oak alleged that letters of this sort were sent out without any intention of attempting reciprocation.[51]

Letters sent by Bancroft and others in the Bancroft's Works department were frequently much more personal than the above, however. The publisher tried to maintain through correspondence the impression, which he had cultivated in his journeys, of concern with individuals. He believed that the department could retain subscribers by showing an interest in them, an attitude which he expressed to Nathan Stone in a letter written less than a year after the campaign for the *Works* began.

Saltillo [Coahuila, Mexico]

Dear Stone

I don't know what course you adopt with regard to writing your subscribers occasionally—I mean having a nice letter written to them—but the continuance of the sets here in Mexico will depend largely upon how they are looked after from San Francisco.

What they want is occasionally a nice letter, speaking a good word, not long—but something that will make them feel that we remember them in some other way than simply the price of a volume.

For instance you could put in a word at first saying that I was much pleased with the manner in which my request for information was met by them, etc.

Another time say something else, —send them a marked paper and then write a few lines saying so, and that you hope the work is giving them satisfaction. . . .

[50] Hectographed form letter found in "Scrapbook of Materials about Hubert Howe Bancroft, his Works, and the Bancroft Library."

[51] Oak, *"Literary Industries" in a New Light*, 18.

> I believe a good letter writer will save the Dept. hundreds of orders that
> would otherwise be dropped.
>
>   HHB[52]

The department found its good letter writers in Richard D. Faulkner and David R. Sessions. Both were college graduates, and both
were to go on, after the period of their employment with Bancroft,
to professional careers—Faulkner in education and Sessions in law.[53]

Sessions, the older of the two, left a position as State Superintendent of Public Instruction in Nevada to join Bancroft's staff in February 1885[54] and worked initially at taking some of the burden of
public relations from Bancroft and Stone. In October he was in New
York, talking to newspaper and periodical editors in an effort to
secure a better coverage for the *Works*. From there he wrote Henry
Oak to ask him to write an article on Bancroft's methods for Dr. Kinsley Twining, literary editor of the *Independent*.[55] In February 1886
Sessions was attempting to control the revolt among Montana subscribers by protesting the wrongs done Bancroft by his canvassers.
In a long letter which was published in the Helena *Weekly Independent*, he stated that the firm knew "to what extent the people of your
territory were imposed upon" by dishonest agents, and declared that
it would be "the happiest epoch in the history of our firm ... could
we secure the conviction and imprisonment in the penitentiary of
those rogues who have bilked us out of thousands of dollars. ..."[56]
Sessions concluded by alleging that the firm had been working towards this goal and expected to have one or more men lodged in the
state prison. There is no trace of this threat being carried out, and
subscribers in Bozeman were drafting resolutions against the Bancroft agents in May.[57]

[52] Bancroft to Stone, September 13, 1883, [History Company Records].
[53] R. D. Faulkner, obituary, San Francisco *Chronicle*, March 21, 1935; D. R.
Sessions, obituary, San Francisco *Chronicle*, January 20, 1924.
[54] *Stone v. Bancroft*, 83. Testimony of D. R. Sessions. Also, *History of Nevada*
(Oakland: Thompson and West, 1881), 226.
[55] Sessions to Oak, October 25, 1885, in Oak, "Correspondence and Papers."
[56] Helena *Weekly Independent*, February 25, 1886.
[57] Bozeman *Weekly Avant Courier*, May 13, 1886.

John Dewey Library
Johnson State College
Johnson, Vermont

Faulkner had attempted to pacify the Montana subscribers in 1884. The opening sentence of the letter in which Bancroft accepted his offer to make the attempt shows the esteem the older man had for his fledgling clerk: "Dear Faulkner, It is exactly what I felt ought to be done, for you or me to go to Montana."[58] The young man had been with the firm only a year at this time, and was usually engaged in expediting communications between the library and the printing shop. In several situations requiring initiative, firmness, and tact, however, he acted as Bancroft's representative. After his trip to Montana, Faulkner went to Washington Territory as a company representative in December of 1884. From April 1885 to January 1887 he was not employed by Bancroft, but after his return he was sent to Mexico City to reorganize the office which Bancroft had opened there after his journey of 1883.[59]

Bancroft had the misfortune to be swindled out of much of the money which the set made in Mexico when the manager of this office, Antonio Urrea, pocketed the receipts, borrowed money from the Mexican government on Bancroft's account, and absconded, deserting his family. Bancroft alleged to Faulkner that it had cost him $5,000 to find out that Urrea was a "natural and first-class scoundrel."[60] Giving the young clerk power of attorney, Bancroft wrote members of the Mexico staff that Faulkner's directions were to be carried out. In a letter sent to Faulkner, Bancroft includes a request that he see a good criminal lawyer and take steps for the immediate prosecution of Urrea.[61]

Less dramatic letters and memoranda from Bancroft to Faulkner include several requests to check matter for the printers, such as footnotes and title pages, and inquiries as to pamphlets Faulkner was writing. One of Faulkner's principal duties during his first term of em-

[58] Bancroft to Faulkner, November 26, 1884, [History Company Records].

[59] Faulkner's general activities and movements are documented by a series of letters and memoranda directed to him by Bancroft and others. Donated to the Bancroft Library by the Faulkner estate, they are in [History Company Records].

[60] All information from letter, Bancroft to Faulkner, October 11, 1887, [History Company Records].

[61] Ibid.

ployment with Bancroft was to try to secure favorable press notices and to circulate them to agents and subscribers. The letters which Bancroft wrote to him not only display Faulkner's responsibilities, but also clearly show Bancroft's intense interest and participation in every phase of the publication and sale of his work.

CHAPTER VII

PUBLICITY AND CRITICAL APPRAISAL

BANCROFT HAD shown his belief in the power of favorable press notices by his own efforts to secure them for the *Native Races*. Agents were advised in a sales manual prepared for this work to seek out newspaper editors, to give them a selection of notices prepared by the Bancroft staff, and to offer free copies of the books for publishing the articles. The manual argues:

> They will almost invariably do it [accept the volume and print the notice]; for in the first place they will see that they are serving their country in endorsing you and the work, in the next place it will be good and interesting reading, and in the third place it will save them the trouble of writing the articles themselves.[1]

The successes of agents for the *Native Races* in placing articles in newspapers led the company to further efforts to provide editors with copy as the *History* was published. Occasionally articles were sent out printed in the form of a newspaper column, making easy work for the newspaper compositor. Early releases were general, concerning the *Works* as a whole, Bancroft's career and methods, and the Bancroft library, which had been moved into a specially constructed building on Valencia Street in 1881. After reviews of

[1] [*Strictly Private*], 1–3. "Scrapbook of Materials about Hubert Howe Bancroft, his Works and the Bancroft Library."

the early volumes began to appear, those which were favorable
were widely distributed.

Bancroft was particularly anxious to place stories in western papers
in order to stimulate sales of the history in the area where the work
would be of greatest interest. His letters to Faulkner and Stone are
filled with advice to both of them on the matter. A series of letters in
February and March 1884 gives the history of one such news story.

While resting at Nordhoff, California, in February 1884 after his
return from Mexico, Bancroft prepared an interview for John P.
Young, managing editor of the San Francisco *Chronicle*. Faulkner
may have proposed the interview; Bancroft wrote to thank him for
suggestions and promised to be ready for Young "as soon as I
arrive."[2] Before he returned to San Francisco, however, Bancroft
dispatched material for the *Chronicle* and asked Faulkner to suggest
that Young write an editorial on it: "if it is all worth anything at all,
it is worth the editor's calling attention to it. . . .If they do it up in
good shape, buy 500 copies of the paper."[3]

The article, "The Mexico of Today," occupied over two columns
on the editorial page of the *Chronicle* of March 22, 1884. In an
adjoining column, a short editorial paragraph commended the interview to readers. Bancroft immediately ordered Faulkner to send
copies to several individuals in California, Utah, and Mexico.[4] A
month later, possibly moved by sales returns, he graciously thanked
Faulkner for his part in the affair: "The interview article was certainly a great success, and its existence was due wholly to you."[5]

Although Bancroft was well pleased with the notice when it
appeared, he had entertained some doubts as to its reception. His mis-
givings were caused by an inner conflict between his interest in the
history as author and as publisher. This letter which he sent to Nathan Stone expresses the dilemma and shows the publisher victorious:

Dear Stone
    If there is anything in this stuff prepared for the *Chronicle* which you

[2] Bancroft to Faulkner, February 3, 1884, [History Company Records].
[3] Bancroft to Faulkner, February 15, 1884, [History Company Records].
[4] Bancroft to Faulkner, March 22, 1884, [History Company Records].
[5] Bancroft to Faulkner, April 26, 1884, [History Company Records].

think will damage the interests of the history you can take it out.

But in this connection it might be well to consider if we are always to keep our mouth shut in matters of rascality, unjust monopoly, or other tyranny.

You are the one to decide, however. I don't want to injure your canvass, but I shall have to let myself out sometime. And it seems to me that against these things is going to be the popular side, and they are the meanest class of men we have had anything to do with etc. etc.

HHB

I don't hit anybody in particular very hard here; how would it do to let this go out as a feeler? ... I don't want to stir up enemies just now, but as I come to modern times my work will be very namby-pamby if I am not allowed to hit vice, wickedness, and swindling as hard as I can.

But you can judge better than I.[6]

In matters where there was no conflict of interest, Bancroft showed no hesitancy in directing the preparation of publicity. Many of his communications are detailed in their directions for the preparation of articles for Colorado, New Mexico, Texas, and other western states. In a letter written a few days after the one quoted above, the historian gave Stone instructions to be passed on to Faulkner:

When I was in Austin I saw the correspondent of the Galveston *News*, the best paper in the state, and spoke to him about a general article, 2000 or 3000 extra copies to be sent direct from the office (the article first being marked) direct [*sic*] to a list of leading men throughout the state which Lucy was to make out and hand in to them.

Will you ask Mr. Faulkner to make up such an article, compile it from other articles, a bang up one covering the entire ground, Library, method, biographical notice of the author (very short) and brief review of some of the Vols ... (he knows what is wanted) include the special matter on Texas which I sent for the revision of the pamphlet and anything else about Texas he thinks of—throw in the word Texas in place of Mexico, Cent. Am, Cal, [*sic*] Oregon, as I have done in the revision of the pamphlet (the Galveston man said make it appear as much as possible of special interest to Texas)—the whole to be 2½ or 3½ ordinary newspaper columns and have it written out neat and clean (after he has prepared it) on foolscap, on one side only.

This will be all ready for Lucy, or if Lucy does not put in an appearance, for whoever takes the agency, for if we add Texas to our territory

[6] Bancroft to Stone, February 15, 1884, [History Company Records].

in the way I suggested we are not going to have any trouble about getting a good agent if we can get any agent for any place. [in margin] If
you and Oak conclude that it is all right to add Texas to title of *North
M. States* how would it do to write Lucy and tell him so, saying that
it doubles his chances.[7]

Both Lucy and the Galveston *News* must have disappointed Bancroft. The agent's name appears in no other letters or records, and
there are no clippings from the newspaper before one in January
1885 announcing the arrival in Galveston of L. Leadbetter and J. G.
Kennedy to gather material for the history.[8]

Bancroft was not to be discouraged by lack of response from one
paper. In October of 1884 he wrote Faulkner that he had placed
general articles in two important Colorado papers, the *Tribune Re-
publican* and the *Rocky Mountain News*, and asked Faulkner to
direct the composition of two or three more articles: "you can designate what they shall take out of the scrapbook and have it all copied."
The same letter told Faulkner just what Bancroft expected: "We
want articles now that will tell the whole story from beginning to
end, with some description of the books and their contents, as well
as of the library and collection, all so that it will be interesting and
easily understood, and all with plenty of praise."[9]

On the following day, Bancroft wrote again:

Mr. Faulkner:
    The articles I made read bang up. [*sic*] I wish you would make up a
dozen or 15, and always have some on hand to place in the hands of
agents going into new fields. The papers almost anywhere will publish
them simply for the asking. These articles were absolutely essential to
the success of the agent here [Denver], and the same will apply I believe
to the solicitation in Wyoming, Texas, Canada and all new country. You
must remember that as we get away from Cal. and the Pacific coast our
works are less known, and we have to make them known and create a
feeling in their favor, and this can be done best by newspaper articles. . . .[10]

---

[7] Bancroft to Stone, February 18, 1884, [History Company Records].
[8] Galveston *Daily News*, January 24, 1885.
[9] Bancroft to Faulkner, October 19, 1884, [History Company Records].
[10] Bancroft to Faulkner, October 20, 1884, [History Company Records].

The letter continues with advice to Faulkner on adding material to the Bancroft articles by including local allusions in the manner Bancroft had recommended earlier. The writer concluded with a reaffirmation of confidence in his articles, "And they read first rate."

The San Francisco papers reviewed the early volumes of the *History*, usually favorably, and Bancroft showed great concern that the reviews be distributed effectively. In a letter that he wrote to Faulkner from Denver, the historian acknowledged receipt of reviews published in the *Chronicle* and the *Argonaut* of the *History of the Northwest Coast*, saying that the *Chronicle* review was "magnificent, just what we want." The letter directs Faulkner to send copies of the *Chronicle* to "Leadbetter's subscribers in Utah, the leading men in Montana, Hatch's subscribers, and the men I have seen in Colorado," and adds to these the names of thirty-five citizens of Wyoming, ten residents of Denver, and a judge living in Council Bluffs, Iowa.

The letter concludes with a bit of practical psychology and an admonition to industry:

> A good notice like that in the *Chronicle* sent to a man who has just subscribed and didn't want to and is a little weak-kneed about it still, will do him lots of good, and make him feel that he hasn't been swindled. I hope you bought 1000 copies of that number.... With 5 or 6 reviews like that of the *Chronicle* before you to cut up or have copied, by various combinations, and throwing in a little local, [*sic*] saying a good word for the agent etc., you can make 12 of them [notices for publication] in 2 hours, barring the copying which can be done by a boy. There is no such thing as not having time to do anything if one only thinks so.[11]

A scrapbook kept by members of the Bancroft staff shows that the *History* was being supported by the metropolitan papers he esteemed most highly ("Really the *Argonaut, Chronicle*, and *Bulletin* settle the matter on the Pacific Coast"),[12] but at the time he wrote this letter few reviews had been published in California except for those in San Francisco papers. The book is filled with clipped articles concerning the *Works* and contains over 700 pages of notices dating from

[11] Bancroft to Faulkner, November 13, 1884, [History Company Records].
[12] Ibid.

1875 to January 1887. The album also contains handwritten notes
which are records of unclipped articles containing the same material
as a notice which has been clipped, e.g. " 'Mountain Tribune,' Bie-
ber, Cal. May 8/86 Published entire Bulletin review of California
IV." Clippings and notes appear approximately in chronological
order, apparently as the information was received. The scrapbook
is full, and the record was probably continued in a second volume
which has not been preserved.[13]

The articles themselves often demonstrate by their similarities a
common source. The paragraph below, one of the more striking
eulogies of Bancroft, appeared as part of several notices published in
1882. The Virginia City *Territorial Enterprise* printed it on October
11, the Chicago *Times* on November 4, and the Philadelphia *Inquirer*
on November 13. On March 31, 1883, it was used in an article in
Frank Leslie's Illustrated Paper.

> In the earlier part of his career he was, like Grote, essentially a man of
> business. His literary labors, at the first were a graceful relaxation from
> the sterner pursuits of active mercantile life. But in due time they became
> so absorbing as to win him almost wholly from business, and then he
> found himself embarked in an enterprise as far surpassing in scope his
> of Grecian renown as the sylvan giants of California might overshadow
> the olive groves of Athens.[14]

This extract demonstrates those qualities of style in the early volumes of the *History* which attracted the scorn of critics. Two reviews of the first volume of the *History of Mexico* characterized
Bancroft's style as: "more appropriate to Mrs. Radcliffe or Ouida
than to history," and "overloaded with extravagance of expression
and robbed of all dignity by the crudeness of its rhetoric."[15] These
harsh verdicts and others equally harsh are pasted side by side with
paens of praise from the *Chronicle* and the *Argonaut*, scissors-and-

---

[13] "Criticisms on H. H. Bancroft's Works. A Collection of Newspaper Clippings,
1878–1887." A reasonably careful examination of the scrapbook shows it to have
been maintained by several people and makes its function obvious.

[14] Ibid., 52–53, 79, 87–88, 167.

[15] First quotation from San Francisco *Evening Bulletin*, February 24, 1883;
second from Syracuse *Herald*, April 29, 1883.

paste reviews from smaller papers, and polite applause from the *Critic*, the *Dial*, the *British Quarterly Review*, and other august, independent journals. The scrapbook is a record, and, if the record is generally a sunny one, it probably reflects the climate of current opinion toward the *Works*.

Occasionally absurdly extravagant praise was showered on Bancroft from unlikely quarters. The New Orleans *Times-Democrat* published only one article, but it seems enough: "It is not our purpose to review the book . . . but simply to call local attention to one of the grandest, largest, most majestic, most generous and most literary undertakings ever attempted not merely in the United States or in modern times, but in the world and during the whole course of civilization."[16] An editorial in the Augusta (Georgia) *Chronicle* proclaimed that Hubert Howe Bancroft was greater than George Bancroft and had God's guidance.[17] The *Texas Baptist Herald* and the Waco *Guardian* carried this comment by Dr. B. H. Carroll: "It is idle to compare with this mammoth enterprise the productions of Herodotus, Thucydides, Livy, Tacitus, Rollin, Gibbon, Hume, Alison, or any other disciple of Clio."[18] Such extravagances were not confined to the South. A review by the Salt Lake *Tribune* of *California* V (published four months after the Bancroft building burned in 1886) eulogizes the period 1847–1848 in these terms: "These two years are to history what John the Baptist was to mankind." The review leaves the reader to speculate on the implications of its analogy without further explanation, and says of the book: "It is worthy to have come as though first tried by fire, for it is pure gold."[19] It is clear that the Bancroft rhetoric found a few responsive ears.

Many reviews came from the Bancroft office, and this kindness is naively acknowledged in at least one case. On May 1, 1886, the Oceanside (California) *Star* thanked A. L. Bancroft and Company for publications furnished by them containing reviews. Usually the smaller papers borrowed review material from larger neighbors with-

16 New Orleans *Times Democrat*, November 7, 1889.
17 Augusta (Georgia) *Chronicle*, November 12, 1886.
18 *Texas Baptist Herald* (Austin), February 11, 1886, quotes Waco article.
19 Salt Lake *Tribune*, September 16, 1886.

out acknowledging any intermediation from the company. It is impossible to separate reviews printed from company releases from those independently borrowed, as this information was not recorded.

In the second half of the scrapbook maintained by the staff, beginning in May 1885, clippings and notes are numbered according to their source, each paper or magazine being assigned a number. In the few cases where no number appears, there is frequently the notation, "See beginning of ledger." This portion of the book, therefore, appears to be part of a system for keeping track of an exchange between the Bancroft's Works department and the journals. The department's share of the exchange must have been the provision of review copies with accompanying promotional material as written by Bancroft, Faulkner, and others. The numbers were probably assigned to the recipients of material to make it easier to gauge returns. If the department were willing to furnish a book, a review, and related material, it seemed only reasonable to expect the newspaper to publish one of the proffered articles or an independent review in exchange.

Few notices appear in the book for 1884, and some articles published in 1884 are not included, although they appear in other scrapbooks. The idea of using the book as a systematic record of press response instead of a repository from which articles might be made up by Faulkner and others may not have occurred to anyone in the department before 1885. In 1884 newspapers were full of the Blaine-Cleveland presidential contest, and editors needed no articles or reviews concerning the *Works* to make up their pages. Review copies continued to go out to newspapers, however. Some control of the distribution of these volumes was necessary, and the scrapbook became a sort of journal or daybook.

Unfortunately the lack of sales records makes it impossible to judge whether the subscription rate responded to changes in publicity techniques which appear in the scrapbook. Clippings show only where agents were active, and what kind of items editors thought newsworthy or entertaining.

However, the articles indicate what the company was attempting to do, and, even though not all notices published in 1884 or earlier were clipped, the record of the book reflects the direction of the campaign. From population centers, concentration of the sales effort moved into the hinterlands. From a general appeal on behalf of Bancroft's grand scheme directed to a would-be intellectual elite, publicity descended to a stress on the entertaining stories in individual volumes in an attempt to attract subscriptions from farmers and small-business men.

Although unsegregated in the book, the articles fall into three classes: (1) General articles concerning the *Works* as a whole, the Bancroft library as source and workshop for the history, or the historian himself and his methods; (2) Reviews or extracts of reviews of specific volumes; (3) Articles prepared by the staff on individual volumes. The last class consists of circulars or portions of circulars considering the contents of the volume as a whole and anecdotes drawn from a page or two in the work.

With very few exceptions, for example, two items from the San Francisco *Chronicle* concerning the visit of the Crown Prince of Japan to the library in January 1883, and two notices from Montana papers concerning dissatisfied subscribers, general articles carry information which could have come only from Bancroft and his staff. Most were prepared by staff members and sent out, unsolicited, to the papers or periodicals which published them, as Bancroft's correspondence with Stone and Faulkner indicates.

General articles appeared less frequently in newspapers than did reviews, as the Bancroft story could be incorporated into the latter. In the East, only thirty-five articles were used by editors after the first three volumes of the *History of the Pacific States* were published, according to the record in the scrapbook, although one hundred and eighty reviews of various volumes appeared to January 1887. In the West, general articles were heavily used in Texas and in small-town California papers in the last half of 1885 and in 1886. Their appearance usually indicates that a canvass is underway, as agents preferred to introduce themselves in a new area with an account of the whole history or the resources of the library, rather than with a review of a single volume.

Reviews were not printed by many western papers until after the publication of *Mexico* V, and San Francisco newspapers published more reviews than were published by any other western papers to that time. This was probably due to the fact that in the 1880s, San Francisco had a population of over two hundred thousand while no other California city had a population of more than forty thousand. Although the small-town newspapers had no literary pretensions, editors were generally friendly, and from May 1885, when the system of assigning numbers to reviewing media went into effect, reviews and articles published in small-town papers outnumbered those publshed in San Francisco.

In March 1885 at the time of publication of *Mexico* V, the Bancroft's Works department began to prepare and mail out stories consisting of passages from individual volumes. The origin of this class of article is made clear in the scrapbook, where it is customary to find only one copy of each article and many pen notes referring to subsequent publication. Notes are written in the following style: "The Bismarck Tribune (M.T.) [Montana Territory] 12–5–86 published our article 'Scrap of Sonoma History' See 669 SB."[20] The text of the article, clipped from the *Daily Democrat* (Santa Rosa, California) of November 10, 1886, appears on page 669 of the scrapbook as indicated.

Nearly fifty different anecdotes were published, most of them drawn from *California* V and *Oregon* I. Nineteen accounts of the Donner party were printed, making the tragedy the leading single subject. Other stories were colorful or humorous. "Life at Old Fort Vancouver," an account of the rough and lively fur trading post taken from *Oregon* I, was used fourteen times; none of the others appear more than eight times. The anecdotes were more popular with western editors than general articles or reviews and over two hundred appearances of this type of article were recorded in the scrapbook.

Although California communities other than San Francisco published about one-third of all articles appearing in the West after March 1885 no division of these communities (by geography, popu-

20 "Criticisms on H. H. Bancroft's Works . . . ," 692.

lation or wealth) yields meaningful results. Fewer articles appeared south of the Tehachapis than in the Sierra region or the Sacramento Valley, but some northern regions were unrepresented. There was no relation between number of articles published in a county and its size or wealth. The department and its canvassers were apparently pleased with all notices, and they left no record of unsuccessful campaigns.

There is no further systematic record of the campaign to maintain press notice, but other scrapbooks in Bancroft Library contain reviews of the later works in the larger city papers. The tone of the selected reviews varies with the viewpoint of the selector. Some collections of reviews were compiled by Bancroft for his children, and one was collected by a person or persons unknown from the more scurrilous writings of his detractors.

An examination of the leading critical journals of the period shows that the *Atlantic*[21] and the *Critic*[22] accorded a few notices to the *History* to the publication of *Alaska* in 1886 and ignored the *Works* thereafter. The *Dial* published one review of moderate length and nine "Briefs" concerning different volumes, all friendly in tone.[23] The *Nation* gave Bancroft more space than the *Atlantic* and the *Critic*, but some of this attention could not have been welcome. On January 25, 1883, the *Nation* reviewed *Central America* I, disparaging Bancroft's authorities.[24] In its next issue the magazine published a letter which charged that Bancroft had not written history but had hired writers to do it for him.

Charles Phelps, author of the letter, had been the editor of the *Californian*, a San Francisco literary magazine, for the first few months of its existence. After a long passage exposing Bancroft's historical method, the letter continued with the allegations that Ban-

[21] *Atlantic Monthly*, L (December, 1882), 859; LIV (July, 1884), 141; LVII (May, 1886), 691–693.

[22] *Critic*, II (December 30, 1882), 353–354; VIII, new series V (February 13, 1886), 79; VIII, new series V (April 24, 1886), 202–203.

[23] *Dial*, VI (November, 1885), 176; (March, 1886), 303; VII (May, 1886), 21; (October, 1886), 132; (March, 1887), 273; VIII (July, 1887), 70; (September, 1887), 101; (April, 1888), 298; IX (September, 1888), 103; X (March, 1890), 315.

[24] *Nation*, XXXVI (January 25, 1883), 85–87.

croft's agents had offered information on the volumes to the San Francisco press "with the intimation that friendly notices would be rewarded," and that Bancroft had assured Phelps that he was "willing to pay liberally for favorable reviews in any respectable paper."[25]

Bancroft took up the gauntlet in a letter published in a later edition of the *Nation*. He reiterated that his work was too vast for one man, and that he had to employ assistants. Bancroft then claimed that at least one-half of the manuscript thus far completed had been written by his own hand, and the remainder had been "so thoroughly revised and rewritten by me . . . as to make it my own." This was not true, and he backed down in the next sentence: "I do not rewrite what is perfectly satisfactory to me merely for the sake of rewriting; I can employ my time and strength to better advantage."[26] The letter continued to explain that Bancroft had been candid from the first about his use of assistants. (He had given his own version of the work assigned to his assistants in the Preface to *Native Races*.) Bancroft concluded with a flat denial of Phelps' "silly charge" of his having offered to pay any newspaper or journal for publicity.[27]

Mr. Phelps retorted in a letter to the New York *Evening Post*, accusing Bancroft of quibbling on the word "offer" and maintaining the truth of his original statement—that Bancroft had told him personally that he was willing to pay for favorable reviews. Phelps expressed shock at Bancroft's practice of offering copies to editors for reviews and closed his letter by remarking that Bancroft agents were besieging San Francisco and New York papers with material about the *Works*.[28]

The *Nation* took no editorial notice of the controversy, but neither did it take further notice of the *Works* until 1885. In a generally favorable review of *Mexico* V published in October of that year, the *Nation* called its discussion of the war between the United States and Mexico the best yet written. The reviewer objected, however, to the

[25] Ibid. (February 1, 1883), 103.
[26] Ibid. (February 15, 1883), 144.
[27] Ibid.
[28] New York *Evening Post*, February 14, 1883. Bancroft's letter had been carried in the *Post* of February 13. The *Nation* was at this time the weekly magazine of the *Post*.

publisher's plea that purchase of the volume was a solemn paternal duty, dismissing the sentiment as ridiculous and regrettable.[29] In later issues the *Nation* carried reviews of *Alaska*, and five subsequent volumes.[30] The review of *Alaska* vindicated Bancroft's use of assistants by saying that it was "difficult to devise other methods by which the desired result could be accomplished in a lifetime."[31] The subject of methodology does not arise in other reviews.

The responses of the major critical magazines show their individuality. The *Atlantic* and the *Critic* wrote primarily for a "literary" audience without the interest in western history or the patience to wade through Bancroft's eight-hundred-page octavos. The *Nation*'s interests were less restricted, and the *Dial*, published in Chicago, was closer to the scene. Both the latter attempted to do justice to the *Works*, after the shock waves generated by Mr. Phelps had died down.

By 1885 the eastern magazines had recovered from this shock of realization that Bancroft's assistants had a share in the *Works* that probably never would be fully acknowledged. Many were curious to know as much as Bancroft chose to divulge. David Sessions in a letter to Henry Oak wrote of this interest and stated of one magazine editor, Dr. Kinsley Twining: "He would use it [information on methodology] for us, now, where 18 months ago he would have used it to condemn." Sessions stated further: "Fact is Mr. Bancroft's methods are his glory in East among critics at present."[32] In the light of the response of the leaders in literary criticism, glory seems a strong word —but there was acceptance.

If the periodicals of the East had warmed toward Bancroft, the literary arbiter of the West had not. The *Overland Monthly*, a continuation of the *Californian* under a new name and editor, published an article on Bancroft in January 1883, and reviews of *Central Amer-*

---

[29] *Nation*, XLI (October 1, 1885), 283–284.

[30] Ibid., XLII (February 11, 1886), 134–135; XLIII (July 29, 1886), 99–100; XLIV (January 13, 1887), 39–40; XLVI (June 14, 1888), 492; XLIV (April 28, 1887), 367–368.

[31] Ibid., XLII (February 11, 1886), 134–135.

[32] Sessions to Oak, October 24, 1885, in Henry L. Oak, "Correspondence and Papers." Bancroft Library.

ica I and *Mexico* I in February and April.[33] The review of *Mexico* I was critical of Bancroft's florid style, and compared his method to that of a newspaper editor rather than a conventional historian. After April there was complete silence. In August 1886 the *Overland* reviewed Josiah Royce's volume on California in the *American Commonwealths* series without mentioning Bancroft; in October of the same year Hittell's *History of California* was reviewed, again without mentioning Bancroft's *History*.[34]

The only clue to this unnatural silence is a remark in an article protesting against literature which was written for advertising and presented as disinterested: "As a matter of fact, not a sentence in the body of the *Overland* is paid for, and any article that is, goes to the advertising pages."[35] Whether or not Bancroft had asserted his willingness to pay for notices, the *Overland* must have been well aware of the gossip. In its zeal to maintain its literary purity before the world, it chose to overlook the important and exhaustive productions of Valencia Street.

Phelps' charge that the *History* was being written by the literary assistants brought forth a few protests from newspapers friendly to Bancroft and a delighted hoot from the *Wasp*, a San Francisco satirical weekly. The *Wasp* had printed the same charges in a discussion of the *History* published in the column "Prattle" on November 11, 1882. The column accused Bancroft of having his work "heralded by 'favorable' notices of interminable length paid for by the line," but said a more serious charge was that Bancroft was not an author but an employer of hack writers: "These gentlemen not only collect his data and digest them; they write his chapters. He transcribes their work and so makes it his own. If this is authorship, the copyists employed by the County Clerk are all authors."[36]

"Prattle" reprinted Phelps' letter and alleged that Bancroft had sent one of his employees to Phelps twice to effect a reconciliation.

[33] *Overland Monthly*, second series, I (January, 1883), 104; I (February, 1883), 200; I (April, 1883), 433–434.
[34] Ibid., VIII (August, 1886), 222; VIII (October, 1886), 447.
[35] Ibid., XIII (March, 1889), 331.
[36] *Wasp*, IX (November 11, 1882), 709.

This statement preceded a specific charge that the *Argonaut* and the *Bulletin* took money for publishing reviews written by Bancroft's staff.[37] "Prattle" was written by Ambrose Bierce, a brilliant and bitter satirist, who had worked for the San Francisco *News Letter* and the *Argonaut*. In 1881 he began work for the *Wasp*, one of the first newspapers to feature topical cartoons in color, and for several years virtually wrote the paper.[38]

Bierce attacked all posturing and hypocrisy fiercely, and few public figures escaped. He may have learned of the Bancroft workshop from Bancroft's ex-assistant T. A. Harcourt as early as 1877, when he and Harcourt collaborated on a revision of William Rulofson's *Dance of Death*, a mocking diatribe against the waltz.[39] Bierce had no occasion to use the information until Bancroft published again, but once the *History* began to come out, the *Wasp* stung Bancroft regularly.

Proxy authorship, Bancroft's clumsy similes, Bancroft's work on the Díaz biography, all were targets repeatedly for Bierce's bludgeon.[40] The visit of historian James Anthony Froude to San Francisco occasioned a report of an imaginary confrontation between him and Bancroft. Froude, expressing astonishment at Bancroft's asking him how much he pays his assistants, receives a haughty reply:

> Sir you are looking at a businessman. Do you think I find time to write histories? Why who would attend to the press-room, etc. etc. . . . Sometimes I look over their manuscript to dot their "i's" and cross their "t's," and if I put my name on the cover, who, I'd like to know, has a better right? I put up the sugar and they run the game.[41]

Bancroft also inspired the *Wasp*'s cartoonist. The cover of the issue of April 18, 1885, carries a cartoon labeled: "Our Gallery of Cranks, No. 3, The Boss Historian." Bancroft is pictured seated be-

[37] Ibid., X (February 24, 1883), 6.

[38] Carey McWilliams, *Ambrose Bierce, a Biography* (New York: Albert and Charles Boni [c. 1929]), 154.

[39] Ibid., 127. (The conjecture about Harcourt is my own.)

[40] E.g., *Wasp*, X (March 3, 1883), 5, 10; XI (November 3, 1883), 3; XIII (August 9, 1884), 5; XIII (August 23, 1884), 5; XIII (November 22, 1884), 5.

[41] Ibid., XIV (April 25, 1885), 3.

fore an open book gazing into the distance with forefinger to temple while hands and arms labeled "journeyman historian" or "apprentice historian" emerge out of the drapes behind him and write in the book.[42]

Bierce continued to write for the *Wasp* until the spring of 1886, but in July of 1885, a change of publishers silenced his clamor against Bancroft. Before he left the staff, Bierce was to see Bancroft's *Works* applauded in its pages, and to face an editorial by John P. Jackson, his new superior, which must have been humiliating to him. Jackson wrote:

> The small-minded local critics who have heretofore written grudgingly of our home historian, Hubert Howe Bancroft, must have a flesh-creeping feeling of personal diminutiveness as they witness the honor with which he and his are received elsewhere.... When such suns of literature as Bryant, Emerson, Bancroft, Longfellow, Holmes, Whittier, Lowell, Parkman, D. Draper, Warner, Higginson, Howells, Darwin and Carlyle write in admiration of our own Bancroft's magnificent publication, it is fitting that the scratching moles of the pen should hie them to their burrowings. The truth is that the grandeur of this historical series makes it a monument of honor to the Pacific Coast, and one which will keep the author's fame conspicuously bright through coming ages.[43]

It is doubtful whether the *Wasp* reached a large enough audience to influence Bancroft's canvass. There is no mention of Bierce or the *Wasp* in surviving letters by Bancroft or his staff. An irritation would not be mentioned unless it became a threat, but Bancroft railed freely when he felt he had been misused by an important reviewing medium. If Bierce, as he claimed, had brought the authorship situation to Phelps' attention and thus to national notice, he would have had an influence on eastern sales and reviews. Phelps, however, knew Mrs. Victor well enough to ask her for an article on the library months before Bierce's review of *Central America* I.[44] Phelps may have shown Bierce's work to E. A. Godkin, editor of the *Nation*, to support his own contentions, but his letter states merely, "I am credibly

---

[42] Ibid., XIV (April 18, 1885), cover.

[43] Ibid., XV (December 26, 1885), 10.

[44] A handwritten note by Mrs. Victor in her scrapbook following clipping of the article states that Phelps was annoyed with her for not attacking Bancroft. Oregon Historical Society.

informed. . . ."[45] Bierce's writing did not reach a large public until he began work for the San Francisco *Examiner* in March 1887 and by that time Bancroft's canvass, having been in operation nearly five years, was slowing down.

Bancroft never mentioned Bierce and on occasion expressed indifference to the eastern press. After printing charges in the *History of the Northwest Coast* that Washington Irving had taken money from John Jacob Astor for Irving's favorable portrait of the millionaire in *Astoria*, Bancroft wrote Faulkner: "I don't care if it does make the eastern goslin's [*sic*] cackle, they don't buy our books."[46] Reaching the prospective customer was the important function of pamphlets, favorable reviews (prewritten or independent), semi-scholarly articles, or folksy stories. The *Overland*'s coolness must have stung, under the circumstances, far more than the *Atlantic*'s.

Whether any paper received more than a review copy for a notice cannot be settled on the basis of surviving evidence. Phelps' and Bierce's charges appear to have a thread of support in one of Bancroft's letters, but the wording of the letter can be interpreted more than one way. In the same note to Faulkner which regally dismissed the "eastern goslin's," Bancroft wrote: "The *Argonaut* article is worth all it cost, but I think they ought to do a little better; still I would not have you spoil anything by trying to get more."[47] If the "cost" was in currency passing between Faulkner and Frank Pixley, publisher of the *Argonaut*, could Faulkner "spoil anything" by more of the same? But if the "cost" were effort on the part of both Faulkner and Bancroft to win over a reluctant editor, overinsistence might well spoil a hard-won victory.

There was no flavor of victory for Bancroft in the occasion which called forth as spontaneous and generous an assortment of notices in the newspapers of the West as any of his accomplishments. When A. L. Bancroft and Company was completely destroyed by fire in 1886, the press responded to the calamity immediately with articles expressing sincere sympathy toward the firm, appreciation of the history, and concern over its continuation to completion.

[45] *Nation*, XXXVI (February 1, 1883), 103.
[46] Bancroft to Faulkner, November 12, 1884, [History Company Records].
[47] Ibid.

CHAPTER VIII

FIRE AND REORGANIZATION

THE FIRST ALARM was turned in at 3:50 P.M., April 30, 1886. By 5 P.M. the Bancroft building was gutted, and the side and rear walls had fallen on neighboring structures. The fire had begun in the western half of the basement, which had been leased to a furniture store, when one of the clerks knocked a candle into a pile of excelsior. The flames rapidly reached the wooden elevator shaft at the rear of the store, shot up it, and began to spread from the fifth floor through the entire building.[1]

Two mattress workers employed by the furniture company lost their lives, but all Bancroft employees escaped without injury. Nothing was saved from the business, however. The story of the blaze in the San Francisco *Chronicle* shows a loss of over half a million dollars.

Cost of building	$125,000
Mortgage	70,000
Machinery	150,000
Stock	400,000
Pianos	20,000
	765,000
Insurance on building	75,000
Insurance on stock	100,000
	$590,000

[1] San Francisco *Examiner*, May 1, 1886.

The loss was unusually severe because Albert Bancroft had used poor judgment. Annoyed by rising insurance costs, he had let $40,000 in insurance on the stock lapse. At the same time, he was tempted by low freight rates to fill the store with paper and other goods.[2]

The Bancroft's Works department suffered heavily. The fire destroyed five or six sets of *History* plates, two thousand volumes of the *History* being prepared for shipment to Mexico, the complete Spanish and English editions of the *Life of Porfirio Díaz*, save for one copy,[3] and all but two copies of the first edition of *Oregon* I, which was in press and in the bindery, being prepared for July release. The copies of *Oregon* I which were not burned had been returned to Mrs. Victor at the library.[4] Sets of plates for a dozen volumes of the *History* were at the library also, as it was the repository for the plates of all volumes after printing.[5]

At the time of the blaze Bancroft was in San Diego, where he had begun to build a summer home for his wife. This city had attracted him since 1870,[6] when he had begun to purchase lots there. The money for these investments had come from his San Francisco bookstore and publishing house, a business which had made him a moderately wealthy man. Income from the store had paid for the library and was expected to carry the *Works* for a few more volumes until they became self-sustaining.

He was distraught, therefore, when he received two telegrams from Nathan Stone telling him that the building was destroyed, and that nothing was saved of the business but the account books. He returned to San Francisco immediately, but was too shaken to leave his house for two days. Although he was able at that time to visit the offices on Geary Street which the staff had rented in the emergency, he was loathe to pass the site of his store for "days and weeks" and during half of that time he confesses to having been sick in bed with

[2] San Francisco *Chronicle*, May 1, 1886.
[3] Ibid. Bancroft Library has the unique copy which escaped the flames.
[4] Caughey, 309.
[5] San Francisco *Evening Bulletin*, May 1, 1886.
[6] San Diego *Union*, September 26, 1886; also, Bancroft, "Personal Observations during a Tour of the Line of Missions in Upper California," 19. According to his own statement, Bancroft bought "about 120 lots in various localities."

"nervous prostration," holding a statement of finances before his eyes until he could not see the figures.[7]

Albert Bancroft, the titular head of the company, had taken the disaster more calmly, but he had little or no capital in the firm. He affirmed that the business would continue as the company had a large warehouse and printing plant at Sacramento and Davis streets. He also placed an advertisement in the same issue of the *Chronicle* which carried the story of the fire. The advertisement states that because of the fire, the company had taken temporary quarters for transacting general business at 110 Geary Street, and that the office of the manufacturing department is located at the top of Sol Wagenheim's Building, "where our Lithographing and Label department has been for the past four years." Orders for printing would be filled promptly as the department had fifteen power presses. The advertisement concludes: "Parties who had unfilled orders at 721 Market will please furnish duplicate copy and instructions to us at our office at Sacramento and Davis Street."

The younger Bancroft continued in orderly fashion to reconstruct. *Publishers' Weekly* on May 8 carried an advertisement stating that the Bancroft business had been destroyed by fire and requesting publishers and manufacturers to mail their catalogs immediately, as well as asking shippers to mail duplicate invoices of rail shipments since March 15 and clipper shipments since December. In the next issue, the magazine carried the same advertisement concerning job printing that had appeared in the *Chronicle*.[8] Meanwhile, Albert prepared the statement of assets and liabilities, which so perturbed his brother, from the rescued account books. Although neither could tell how many of their debts were collectible or how patient their creditors might be, the statement showed an excess of assets of $100,000 over the liabilities. The estimate of fire loss was only $250,000 over the amount covered by the insurance, less than half

[7] Bancroft, *Literary Industries*, 772–774, 776; also Henry Raup Wagner, "Albert Little Bancroft, His Diaries, Account Books, Card String of Events and Other Papers," *California Historical Society Quarterly*, XXIX (December, 1950), 359. Wagner states: "Hubert Bancroft had a nervous breakdown." This seems a severe term for his brief illness.

[8] *Publishers' Weekly*, XXIX (May 8, 1886), 601; (May 15, 1886), 625.

the original figures in the *Chronicle*. Assuming solvency, Albert rented a store on Market Street, left it in charge of T. A. C. Dorland and F. A. Colley, and went east to purchase stock.[9]

Albert's coolness contrasted sharply with his brother's distress. The older Bancroft decribed his intense depression floridly and melodramatically:

> For thirty years I have had a bookstore in this town, and the first and finest one here, or within two thousand miles of the place. Whenever I walked the streets, or met an acquaintance, or wanted money, or heard the bells ring for church, or drove into the park, or drew to the breast my child; whenever I went home at night, or down to business in the morning, or out to my library, or over to my farm, I had this bookstore. And now I have it not. I have none. I never shall have one again. It is I who should have been destroyed, and not this hive of industry which provided food for five hundred mouths.[10]

The prospects for the history looked dark to him. Twenty volumes of the *Works* had been issued, and, though the firm was $200,000 behind on the enterprise, returns were gaining on expenses. To lose these gains was unnerving to Bancroft, who found himself with literally nothing but an expensive library with the plates for twelve volumes of the *Works* in its basement. He resented attempts to comfort him:

> "What a blessing your library was not burned," the old-womanish men would say. "It was providential that you had moved it." Blessing! There was no blessing about it. It was altogether a curse; a cursed and contemptible dispensation of providence, if that is the orthodox term for bad luck. And of a truth I should have felt relieved if the library had gone too, and so brought my illustrious career to a close. I felt with Shylock, as well take my history as take from me the means of completing my history.[11]

There is no reason to suspect his sincerity, nor to doubt the force of the sense of duty which led him away from despair and resignation. "The question was not what I would like to do, but what I ought to

---

[9] Wagner, *California Historical Society Quarterly*, XXIX (December, 1950), 359.
[10] Bancroft, *Literary Industries*, 775.
[11] Ibid., 777.

do."[12] The sentiment is strictly in accordance with his upbringing.

He had a duty to his history and its subscribers, to his business creditors, and to his family. He railed bitterly at his competitors: "I do not know how we all could have gone to work to confer the greatest pleasure upon the greatest number so effectually as in burning up our establishment." He cursed the management of the store: "which unknown to me, had crammed full to overflowing eight large floors with precious merchandise in order to take advantage of low freights, at the same time cutting down on the volume of insurance so that when the match was applied in the basement of the furniture store adjoining . . . the old business should be killed as dead as possible."[13] He also took the first steps toward continuing the history and building a new business.

Bancroft's position was difficult: he had no source of income, and at first rejected the idea of rebuilding, as it had been necessary to mortgage the structure which had burned. When he offered the lot, however, no one would meet what he considered a fair price. It took two months for the new statements of accounts to come in from creditors, and until they came the solvency of the business was in doubt. However, savings banks sent him word that if he "wanted to rebuild to come around and get the money." and he determined to rebuild.[14]

Work on the *History* was resumed after the staff submitted a statement of condition, showing what plates had been destroyed, what writing was to be done, and an estimate of the time and expense needed to complete the work. The estimate was two years and twelve thousand dollars, but Bancroft found that nearly twice as much time and money was required.[15]

There is no hint of the vacillation expressed in Bancroft's autobiography in the circulars sent to subscribers. Someone, presumably Stone, sent out a sheet to subscribers reassuring them that the set would *"positively proceed to completion,"* but that the volume

[12] Ibid., 778.
[13] Ibid., 777 (both quotations).
[14] Ibid., 780–782.
[15] Ibid., 782.

which would have been issued July 20 would be delayed over a month. The notice closes with a request for immediate remittances. It is dated May 3, the day before Bancroft visited his staff on Geary Street. On May 7 a second circular was sent out, declaring that all manuscript of the history was saved, and that material for the manufacture of more volumes had been ordered from the East by telegram.[16] Both notices are printed over the name of A. L. Bancroft & Co., Publishers.

On May 5, this letter was sent to all editors in correspondence with the Bancroft firm. The first paragraph is quite positive:

San Francisco, Cal., May 5, 1886

Dear Sir:

You are aware of the great loss we suffered by the destruction of our publishing house and stock of goods on the 30th of April. We have been clearing away the ruins in order to resume business. Though the shock was severe we are on our feet again. The first branch of the business to be resumed will be the publication of Bancroft's Historical Works. Preparations have been made for this already. The publication will be delayed a few weeks, but after that it will go on to completion as hitherto, and strictly according to the original design.[17]

The second paragraph reviews Bancroft's endeavor and reputation, and points out that the history presents "this part of the United States in its true light to the East and to Europe, from which we desire first-class immigration and capital." The concluding paragraphs ask the editors' cooperation in urging subscribers to send their remittances for volumes which they have received promptly. A few days later, a a letter which had been received from I. D. Farwell of Niles, California, was sent to editors. Farwell had expressed sympathy over the loss from the fire and offered to forward the full amount of his subscription to the *Works*.[18]

This positive, optimistic, purposeful campaign to reassure subscribers and reestablish the history must have been Nathan Stone's

---

[16] Notices from: "Criticisms on H. H. Bancroft's Works. A Collection of Newspaper Clippings. 1878–1887."

[17] Ibid.

[18] Ibid.

work. Albert Bancroft was preoccupied with reestablishing the stationery and book business, and Hubert was suffering from depression and, more practically, taking measures to secure part of his fortune. Certainly, if the older Bancroft became upset when people congratulated him on the security of his library, he could scarcely have been in the frame of mind to write the serenely confident dodgers which were sent out during the first weeks of May. At this time Stone was counted among "the true and noble fellows of our own establishment, who stood by us regardless of any consequences to themselves."[19] He was soon to be rewarded.

By the end of May, Bancroft was again in command of himself and his history, and the decision was made to publish the fifth volume of the *History of California* in place of the destroyed *History of Oregon*, volume I.[20] *California* V had been completed and was to be released in October but publication was rescheduled for August. The migrations of the 1840s, including the Donner party, and the conduct of the Mexican War in California were recounted in it and made it a volume of much more general interest than the two preceding volumes on California. *California* V would be widely reviewed and would certify that the *History* would continue.

A. L. Bancroft & Company, however, was splintered. On May 6, one week after the fire, the Bancroft brothers entered into partnership with Sumner Whitney to found the law publishing firm of Bancroft-Whitney. The law department of A. L. Bancroft & Company was transferred to the new firm, and Albert Bancroft became president. Hubert Bancroft held a substantial portion of the stock,[21] although he realized little on it because the elected officers voted themselves large salaries instead of returning profits in dividends.[22]

Separation of the business enterprises of the two brothers was hastened by a quarrel which severed their personal relations as well.

[19] Bancroft, *Literary Industries*, 783.
[20] *Publishers' Weekly*, XXIX (June 5, 1886), 739; XXX (July 24, 1886), 131.
[21] San Francisco *Journal of Commerce* (August 12, 1886); also Philip Bancroft, "Politics, Farming and the Progressive Party in California," an interview conducted by Willa Klug Baum (Berkeley: University of California General Library, Regional Cultural History Project, 1962), unpublished typescript, 22–23.
[22] Bancroft, *Literary Industries*, 789.

Neither brother made public the date of dispute or the motives behind their difference. It has been blamed on Albert's unfortunate decision preceding the fire, concerning the insurance, and also on Hubert's resentment of his brother, first aroused by a public acknowledgment of the latter's ability four years before.[23] Albert has left a bitter account in typescript in the custody of the Society of California Pioneers; Hubert expunged his brother's name from *Literary Industries*.[24] Their children recall living on adjoining farms in Walnut Creek, their fathers never meeting and rarely speaking of each other.[25]

At the time of the quarrel Hubert was preparing to rebuild and reenter publishing and bookselling actively. Albert would not have wanted to play "little brother" again whether or not he had been invited to. His income at the time of the fire has been estimated by his family at $30,000 a year.[26] Calling his independent firm by the familiar name, A. L. Bancroft and Company, Albert remained in competition with his brother.

[23] Bertha Knight Power, *William Henry Knight, California Pioneer* ([n.p.] 1932), 64, presents the insurance decision as reason for the quarrel. This is a neat theory, but W. H. Knight could have no direct knowledge of the quarrel as he had left A. L. Bancroft and Company in 1879. The story is at least third-hand, and the origin is not given. Wagner in: *California Historical Society Quarterly*, XXIX (September, 1950), 227, advanced the second theory. The article was: "A Cosmopolitan Publishing House," *Paper World*, XII (March 1, 1881), 1–6.

[24] "Then [1870] I changed the name of the business, the initial letters only, my responsibility, however remaining the same" (*Literary Industries*, 162). Bancroft cursed the "management" over the stock-insurance ratio, and mentions the ingratitude of "some...for whom we had done the most" (ibid., 777, 783), both probably with reference to Albert. Albert's name or A. L. Bancroft and Company is never mentioned.

[25] Philip Bancroft, "Politics...," 19. In a telephone conversation with me on May 12, 1966, Philip Bancroft stated that his father maintained that Albert had given false testimony against him, but that his father never discussed the quarrel with his children. Alberta Reid, Albert's daughter, told me that her father felt that Hubert was unfair to him in taking the business out of his hands after the fire (statement taken July 23, 1967). However, A. L. Bancroft and Company continued in business, without Hubert, for some time according to Wagner's article on Albert: *California Historical Quarterly*, XXIX (December, 1950), 359.

[26] Wagner, *California Historical Society Quarterly*, XXIX (September, 1950), 217.

Hubert Bancroft, while uncertain of his solvency, had moved rapidly and effectively to protect his wife and children by placing his revenue-producing San Diego real estate in his wife's name.[27] Assured of his family's security, he created a new corporation. A bank account was opened in the name of the History Company on May 18, 1886.[28] The assets of the new company were outstanding accounts for the history, and remaining plates and stock; the bank account must have been intended to keep payments on the *Works* out of the hands of A. L. Bancroft & Company's creditors.[29] Incorporation papers were filed on September 13, naming five directors or trustees: Hubert Howe Bancroft; his wife, Matilda; Kate Bancroft; Nathan Stone; and Stone's wife, Olive.[30]

Capital was given as $500,000, divided into ten thousand shares, completely subscribed. Bancroft held 8,970 shares valued at $448,500; Stone, 1,000 shares valued at $50,000; and the ladies, 10 shares ($500) each.[31] The capital was somewhat intangible, representing unpaid orders on unpublished books. Bancroft, however, felt "we had an equivalent to it in every way."[32]

The articles of incorporation state that the History Company's purpose was primarily "to manufacture, publish and sell the historical works of Hubert Howe Bancroft." General publishing, lithographing and engraving, and retail book and stationery selling are also included in the very broad statement of purpose.[33] Stone was made vice-president of the new company, given a salary, and put to work

[27] Bancroft, *Literary Industries*, 789–790, 797; San Diego *Union*, September 26, 1886. The *Union* said Bancroft had given his wife half a million dollars' worth of real estate over a period of several years, but Bancroft's account makes it appear that he deeded her much of it after the fire.

[28] *Stone v. Bancroft*, 21. Testimony of N. J. Stone.

[29] Bancroft did not include this account in his estimate of the capital of the History Company, *Stone v. Bancroft*, 164. A large part of it may have been cash borrowed to rebuild.

[30] "Articles of Incorporation of the History Company." California State Archives, Sacramento, California.

[31] Ibid.

[32] *Stone v. Bancroft*, 164. Testimony of H. H. Bancroft.

[33] "Articles of Incorporation of the History Company." California State Archives, Sacramento, California.

at his old job of employing agents for selling the history.[34]

Quarterly publication of the *Works* continued. In contrast with the earlier volumes which had been turned out in haste to meet deadlines, there were several volumes in manuscript and galley at the library waiting their turn to go to press. *Oregon* I was reset to follow *California* V and brought the series back on schedule by appearing in October. All twenty volumes of the *Works*, including the *Native Races*, which had previously been published by A. L. Bancroft and Company, were reissued with the imprint of the History Company, eighteen of them in 1886.[35] Printing was distributed among a number of establishments,[36] binding was done by Hicks-Judd Company, and composition and plates for new or destroyed volumes was done by Fillmer-Stiller Company.[37] The association with the latter company must have been strained when Fillmer-Stiller sued the History Company for nearly $3,000 for materials and labor in May 1887.[38]

By the time of the Fillmer-Stiller suit, one of Bancroft's nephews was in a position to undertake the composition and plate-making if the contract had been permanently ruptured. W. B. Bancroft, who had been in charge of the printing plant in the A. L. Bancroft building, had established a printing business under his own name on First Street after the fire and was succeeding in it.[39]

Bancroft persuaded his nephew to reenter business with him. He had decided, at some time after letting the contracts for his new building to separate the History Company completely from the general bookstore and publishing firm he contemplated conducting. In order to do this, he filed articles of incorporation for the Bancroft Company on June 21, 1887. The statement of purpose includes all of the printing, manufacturing, publishing, and selling clauses which appear in the History Company's papers, except for those having to do with the history. Directors were Bancroft, his daughter, Kate, W. B. Bancroft,

[34] *Stone v. Bancroft*, 22. Testimony of N. J. Stone.

[35] *Mexico* III and *Mexico* V were reissued in 1887.

[36] San Francisco *Journal of Commerce*, August 12, 1886.

[37] Charles H. Shinn, "Early Books, Magazines and Book Making," *Overland Monthly*, second series, XII (October, 1888), 345.

[38] San Francisco *Examiner*, May 10, 1887. The outcome of the suit is unknown.

[39] Bancroft, *Literary Industries*, 798; also Albert Bancroft, "Statement."

Stone, T. A. C. Dorland and F. A. Colley.[40] (Dorland and Colley were long-time employees of A. L. Bancroft and Company, who had remained loyal to the senior Bancroft.)

Capitalization was placed at $550,000, a figure which may have been Bancroft's estimate of the value of his land and the building constructed on it. The 5,500 shares of stock said to be worth $100 a share were divided as follows: Bancroft 2,746 shares, Kate 2,746 shares, with 2 shares apiece to the four other directors. If Stone and the rest did not gain much by such an arrangement, neither did they risk much.

Contracts were let for the new building in August 1886.[41] One year later, Bancroft moved both of his corporations under its roof and announced his return to business. To a correspondent of the New York *Tribune* he affirmed his intention of giving his personal supervision to establishng the largest and finest bookstore west of New York. The correspondent's paragraph, quoted in *Publisher's Weekly* where it would fall under the eye of eastern publishers and wholesalers, closed with the remark: "The great boom in San Diego, where he held much property, has given him ample capital to carry out his plans."[42] The reporter may not have been deliberately misled, but, of course, Bancroft had taken good care to reserve the income from his San Diego properties for his wife and children.

The History Building was opened to the public in August, 1887. In an interview published in the San Francisco *Examiner*, Bancroft explained the name:

> For the past twenty years my efforts have been directed almost exclusively to historical matters, and it is in commemoration of that period now closed that the imposing structure on Market Street has been erected and called the History Building, the pile being intended as a sort of monument.[43]

[40] "Articles of Incorporation of the Bancroft Company." California State Archives, Sacramento, California.

[41] San Francisco *Chronicle*, August 2, 1886.

[42] *Publishers' Weekly*, XXXII (August 6, 1887), 176.

[43] San Francisco *Examiner*, June 15, 1887.

Although Bancroft would have seen nothing incongruous in so commemorating a work which should (and did) outlive its memorial, the name also served to keep the history before the public eye. Despite this effort, less than three thousand more subscriptions were secured after 1886.[44] The cream had been skimmed. The prosperous had been approached, and the interested among them had subscribed. Furthermore, with more and more volumes published, prospective customers found the immediate cost difficult to meet. Charles B. Turrill of San Diego was shipped nineteen volumes of the *Works* in May 1887 and advised that in addition to his initial payment of $20 on April 27, he was to pay $11 per month until "issue was overtaken" and thereafter as published.[45] Terms like these put the complete set out of reach for many.

Others, both subscribers and local critics, were groaning about the stream of books. Those who wanted portions of the whole could write to other San Francisco bookstores to pick up the few volumes in which they were interested. Samuel Carson was ready to oblige. His advertisement in April 1888 offers all volumes of the *History* at $2.25 for cloth, $3.00 for leather, and remarks as follows:

> In lots to suit, one volume or more at a time. Any person buying these books from us at the above prices will not be harrassed to take the balance of the set, whether wanted or not. We do not know (no one does) how many volumes there will be issued, but we presume one hundred and fifty or more volumes will be published at $4.50 each. We will sell them all as they come out at $2.25 retail. Add 30 cents per volume for postage if ordered by mail.[46]

The History Company tried to stir interest by mailing out stories drawn from the volumes to show their readability (Chapter VII). Response of editors was excellent, but there is no indication whether a new wave of sales followed. In 1889 the promises made to early subscribers were broken, and subscriptions for portions of the *His-*

[44] *Stone v. Bancroft*, 200–201. Testimony of H. H. Bancroft.

[45] H. B. Hambly (for History Company) to Turrill, May 4, 1887. Society of California Pioneers.

[46] *Publishers' Weekly*, XXXIII (April, 1888), 640.

tory were taken. One of Stone's letters to Judge Deady told him that the two volumes on the Northwest Coast and the two volumes on Oregon would be sold as two separate sets in Oregon, as the volumes were expected to meet with a large sale there.[47] Impersonal form letters, requesting help in recruiting agents, announce similar plans for the *History of Central America* and the *History of Alaska*.[48]

California Pastoral and *California Inter Pocula* were published in 1888, both separately and as part of the *Works*. In 1890 Bancroft carried through his plan to reissue other volumes in the *Works* as separate regional histories. Several of these, like the *History of California* in seven volumes, were sets in themselves; others like the *History of Alaska* or the *History of Arizona and New Mexico* were single volumes, relatively inexpensive for the subscriber. All of the *Works* except *Native Races* and *Essays and Miscellany* was reissued in this fashion, although the *History of the North Mexican States and Texas* reappeared as the *History of Texas and the North Mexican States*.[49]

The agents selling individual volumes bought the books from the company and had to make deliveries and collections in the manner of salesmen for other subscription works. The profit for the agent was high: 66 percent on cloth or leather, 105 percent on half-morocco and half Russia bindings, and 108 per cent on full morocco.[50] Between June 1889 and May 1890, agents sold over two hundred and thirty volumes each of *British Columbia* and *Utah*, and two hundred volumes of *Texas*. Sales for *Oregon* and *Alaska* were much lower, forty-two and eighty-six copies respectively, but records may not be complete. Most titles were sold in the territories with which they were concerned, but there were exceptions. *Utah* was generally

---

[47] Stone to Deady, March 12, 1889. Oregon Historical Society.

[48] Form letters in: "Scrapbook of Reviews of the Bancroft Publications." Bancroft Library.

[49] Association of Research Libraries, *A Catalog of Books Represented by Library of Congress Printed Cards, Issued to July 31, 1942* (Ann Arbor, Mich.: Edwards Brothers, 1943), v. 9, 223–226.

[50] Agents' lists show the following figures: cloth $2.70, leather $3.30, half morocco $3.90, full morocco $4.80. Prices to the subscriber were, respectively, $4.50, $5.50, $8.00, and $10.00. Agents' figures from: "Agents' Orders for [individual copies of] Bancroft's *Works*," June 9, 1889–May 23, 1890, [History Company Records].

popular, and twenty-five copies of it were ordered by an agent in as remote a place as Tasmania in April 1890.[51]

Revenues from subscribers were coming in, and the History Company was able to pay dividends to its very select group of stockholders, but the Bancroft Company faced competition from Carson and other bookdealers, and Bancroft-Whitney had escaped Bancroft's control.[52] A source of substantial revenue was needed as the History Building bore a heavy mortgage.

Immediately after the fire, Bancroft had taken steps to offer his library to the State. A bill to purchase the library for $250,000 was introduced in the State Senate, and on January 25, 1887, ex-Senator C. W. Cross, of Nevada County, addressed himself to the Senate Committee on the State Library on Bancroft's behalf. After discussing the value of the library to the state, Senator Cross stated that Bancroft had intended either to give his library to the state, or to present it to a university or society where it would be accessible to the public, but that his losses in the fire which destroyed his business obliged him to sell it.[53]

The senator continued, saying that estimates of the value of the collection had been obtained "from all the prominent libraries of the state and the United States, besides estimates from dealers in two large book markets in Europe." The consensus was that the collection was worth $250,000.[54] The senator probably got his information from *The Bancroft Historical Library*, a thirty-eight-page booklet from the press of W. B. Bancroft, which contained a petition to the legislature to buy the library because of its size, value, and pertinence to California. The brief petition was followed by thirty pages of names of endorsees from business and professional circles and an appraisal over the names of eighteen authorities, eight of whom were librarians.[55]

[51] "Agents' Orders for Bancroft's *Works*," June 9, 1889–May 23, 1890, [History Company Records].

[52] *Stone v. Bancroft*, 22. Testimony of N. J. Stone; Bancroft, *Literary Industries*, 788–789.

[53] San Francisco *Evening Bulletin*, January 26, 1887.

[54] Ibid.

[55] *The Bancroft Historical Library*, [San Francisco, 1887(?)], 38 pp.

Opposition to the bill was rigorous. The sum asked was a large one for a collection of limited usefulness, and there were always other uses for state funds. Despite the appraisal, many legislators and their constituents doubted the value of Bancroft's collection. The bill did not pass in 1887 and was reintroduced in 1889. Several San Francisco newspapers expressed outrage. The *News Letter* accused Bancroft of bribery, stating that one-third of the purchase price for the library was to go to legislators voting for the bill, one-third to lobbyists, and one-third to Bancroft.[56] This charge was completely irresponsible and was not taken up by the other journals. The *Examiner* and the *Alta California* were equally indignant at the prospect of the legislature's squandering a quarter of a million dollars on the Bancroft collection. Bierce, now writing for the *Examiner*, termed the collection valueless except as fuel, exclaiming, "The library would not be worth as much to the state as Mr. Hubert Howe Bancroft's brains to an educated pig."[57] Even the staid *Alta California* called the "scheme" to sell the library to the state "impudent," and in a later issue rejoiced that it was to be given its "final quietus" by an adverse report from the Senate Committee on the State Library.[58]

Bancroft, of course, persisted in his efforts to sell the library, and a joint resolution of the Senate and House passed in June 1892 to investigate and report to Congress the value of the Bancroft library indicates that the matter reached Washington.[59] Long before this, however, Bancroft found a new way to use his library, his assistants, and his reputation to recoup some of his fortune and keep his name as a historian before the public.

---

[56] San Francisco *News Letter*, February 2, 1889.

[57] San Francisco *Examiner*, January 27, 1889.

[58] *Alta California* (San Francisco), February 7 and 14, 1889.

[59] *Congressional Record*, 52d Cong., 1st Sess. 23:6 (June 12, 1892), 5365. The House Committee on Library to which the task of appraisal was referred appointed the Chairman of the Senate Committee on Library, the Chairman of the House Committee on Library and the Librarian of Congress to appraise Bancroft's collection. 52d Cong. 1st Sess., H. Rept. 1795. No report of the result was released by the Committee on Library.

CHAPTER IX

A SEQUEL TO THE *WORKS*

WHEN THE LAST volume of the *Works* was published in 1890, Bancroft had already taken orders and collected some material for a series which he planned to present as a sequel to the *History of the Pacific States*. In seeking a source of additional revenue, he employed a formula which was popular in local histories. County histories were commonly published and sold by subscription in the West. Each of these works contained a section of biographies, including engraved portraits of subscribers or pictures of their residences. Bancroft's new work would be the biographical section of his history. and the subjects of the biographies, like those in the county histories, would be charged for an engraved portrait and a narrative of their accomplishments.

Bancroft first became aware of his opportunity to profit from the publication of a vanity biography when his quest for material for the *Pacific Encyclopedia* produced a number of letters from California pioneers eager to see their names in print. His peripatetic assistant, Enrique Cerruti, cautioned him that the pioneers were anxious to have their portraits engraved for the *Encyclopedia* to appear beside their narratives[1]—something Bancroft was not contemplating at the time.

[1] Cerruti to Oak, May 7, 1874, [History Company Records]: "Please tell H. H. to bear in mind that the old settlers *must not be made aware that their mugs are not*

In 1877, however, long after he had abandoned the *Pacific En-*
cyclopedia, he requested Alonzo Phelps, an aging ex-college president who had done some writing on Cuba for Appleton's, to work
on a biography of the pioneers. Phelps received a commission on the
sums, about $250 per plate, which he obtained from patrons for steel
engravings and biographies, as well as the usual author's royalties.[2]
The two-volume work, *Contemporary Biography of California's*
Representative Men, was published in 1881.

Bancroft realized that this work, which had preceded the *History*
and had no connection with it, had fallen far short of exhausting the
market for subsidized biography. Men had subscribed for the *Works*
merely to see their names and deeds in print, and many were probably
dissatisfied with the brief footnotes accorded them. Other subscribers, whose names appeared more prominently, were also unappeased.
Bancroft's friend, Judge Deady, wrote that he was "nettled and
disappointed" by the treatment given him in the history. Mrs. Victor,
who had written the portion of the work in which he figured, replied
that he had been "put to the fore as much as would be proper in a
general history."[3] However, he and many others wanted to see their
accomplishments more fully treated. These customers, who had been
willing to subscribe $175.50 to $390 for notice in the *Works*, would
pay much more handsomely for a biography and portrait in its sequel.

The author of the *History of the Pacific States* did not need the
name of Alonzo Phelps or any other scholar to sell this biography. It
was to be presented to the public as material gathered in the preparation of the history which could not be used because of the require-
ments of space and the disciplines of the form. Only the subjects of
the sketches and the Bancroft staff of writers and salesmen were to

---

needed for the encyclopedia [*sic*] I tell you this much because everyone that visits
me or invites me to his ranch is anxious to have the likeness or portrait *engraved in*
steel! and pasted alongside their narratives."

[2] *Phelps v. Cogswell*. Transcript on Appeal: Superior Court, City and County of
San Francisco. (San Francisco: Bacon, 1883), 35, 39.

[3] Victor to Deady, July 9, 1889. Oregon Historical Society. Mrs. Victor quotes
Deady's protest in her reply.

know that the work would consist largely of new material submitted by the biographees.

The *Chronicles of the Kings* was to be published in a series of octavos designed to match its predecessor in height, breadth, and styles of binding. Bancroft wrote of his enthusiasm for the project to Nemos:

Dear Nemos

Your analysis of the character of Brigham Young and others is very good, short simple and individual, no indiscriminate and lavish praise and no great blame, but the truth. This is the most interesting kind of reading to me, where the man has done something, and all of our men have done something—every one of them has an interesting and important biography. Carried out on the present plan, I do not think I exaggerate when I say that the Chronicles will prove one of the most interesting books of the kind that ever was written, and that it will last throughout all time. And I believe that as men see and understand the work they will be more and more glad to come into it.[4]

In this letter, Bancroft may have been trying to convince himself, as well as Nemos, of the value of what he proposed to do.

The *Chronicles* was written for profit, and some of the longest biographies in the work concern men whom the historian detested. In 1884 Bancroft had written during a visit to Colorado:

The Tabor people here are very bad eggs. Although he is very wealthy and has long been a public [*sic*] he is very generally despised. He put away his wife for some cause and married a disreputable woman. The least said about any of them the better.[5]

But the *Chronicles* devote sixty-seven pages to H. A. W. Tabor, and even more space, one hundred and ten pages, is accorded to Collis P. Huntington, although Bancroft had written in 1884: "I have never met a railroad man who was not the quintessence of meanness in more

[4] Bancroft to Nemos, May 29 [1888 (?)], no. 35.
[5] Hubert Howe Bancroft, "Colorado Notes" (handwritten), 2–3. Bancroft Library.

respects than one."[6] Huntington was no exception in his eyes, as Bancroft's later writings show.[7]

Tabor and Huntington each paid $10,000 to appear in the biography.[8] The *Chronicles of the Kings* charged its patrons a sum that set a record for works of the kind. The minimum entrance fee was $1,000 for a steel portrait and four pages of print.[9]

To understand the measure of success which the *Chronicles* achieved, it is necessary to recall the market. The heterogeneous pioneer society had, with the development of the railroad, the Comstock, and large private landholdings, been transformed to a divided society where capital and labor conflicts were common. Great fortunes had been made and the new multimillionaires were not shy about displaying their prosperity. The Bancroft Company was preparing a California *Blue Book*, the introduction to which stressed that: "A BLUE BOOK has always been deemed an essential adjunct to the literature of every prominent family in the leading Eastern Cities and European Capitals; and its absence here in the past was noticeable. . . ."[10] The "haves" were separating themselves from the "have-nots."

In the mid-eighties, railroads, steamship lines, land companies, and chambers of commerce began a publicity campaign to attract tourists and new settlers to Southern California, and in 1885, fifty thousand homeseekers reached the state. In ten years, 1880–1890, the population of the state rose from 517,000 to 1,200,000. As Bancroft surmised, those who came first wanted to assert their priority. Pioneers

---

[6] Ibid., 2.

[7] Edward A. Dickson, "Bancroft's Lost Letter," *Historical Society of Southern California Quarterly*, XXXV (September, 1953), 216. In this letter, Bancroft termed Huntington "a foul fish"; also, Bancroft, *Retrospection*, 232, 234, 238, pointed out how Huntington, as leader of the "Big Four," helped usher in a "Dark Age of Graft."

[8] Harry B. Hambly, "List of Subscribers to *Chronicles of the Builders of the Commonwealth* Showing Amounts Subscribed and Paid" (typewritten), 1–2. Bancroft Library.

[9] San Francisco *Examiner*, June 12, 1890, 3.

[10] *The San Francisco Blue Book: Being the Fashionable Private Address Directory and Ladies' Visiting and Shopping Guide of San Francisco and Surroundings Containing the Names, Addresses, Reception Days and Country Residences of the Elite of San Francisco, San Rafael, Sausalito, San Mateo, Redwood City, Menlo Park, San Jose, Etc., Etc., Season 1888–89* (San Francisco: Bancroft, 1888), 254, LXVIII [6] pp.

had become the heads of families, were growing old, and were anxious for recognition—for the depression following the coming of the railroad, the popularity of Henry George's *Progress and Poverty*, the labor riots, and the Chinese problem, all pointed to a different society in which their careers could be lost to view and their words unheeded. Bancroft aimed his campaign at their pride and fears.

Bancroft approached his projected work methodically. He first had to find his "kings" in order to offer them a place in his *Chronicles*, and for this purpose he had lists of subscribers to the *Works* prepared. The lists, together with a circular describing the proposed work, were sent to agents in the field with the request that they mark the names of outstanding men in their territories.[11]

Agent L. H. Nichols, at the conclusion of a letter explaining the marks he had chosen to use on the lists which he returned, was mildly critical of the Bancroft approach:

> I judge from the circular that you will include those parties who have by their force and capacity made much money as well as those who became prominent in their sections because of their ability.
> I think there are very few *real Kings* and as a matter of fact I should think you would have to look outside of your lists of subs to make such a book at all complete and this I presume you will do. . . .[12]

Bancroft's reply has not been preserved, but he included in the published *Chronicles* such deceased leaders as Father Serra and Benito Juárez to give the book the required tone. However, he was happy to accept the kingly fee for admission to his hall of fame from any man whose presence would not make the work's pretensions absurd.

After his canvassers had returned their lists with the names of prospective "kings" checked, Bancroft sent these leaders a form letter

[11] Several folders in [History Company Records] contain these handwritten lists of names, headed by the names of Bancroft agents. All lists are written in the same neat clerical hand. There are 2,123 names that appear on the lists that remain. Each name is preceded by an account number and is followed by the name of a city or town and a letter indicating style of binding. Originals are in black ink on yellow ruled paper.

[12] [Nichols to Bahcroft, no date, salutation, or signature.] Pinned to Nichols' lists for Washington Territory, Oregon, and Utah, [History Company Records].

within a brochure. The letter informed the recipient that: "We have placed your name on our list of personages entitled to recognition in our Chronicles of the Kings and you are hereby invited to take your proper place therein." The letter continued, saying that the "greatest care and discrimination" had been used in selecting names, and that the steel plate portraits were "limited" to one thousand.[13] The brochure, bearing on its ivory paper cover simply the initials C and K and a crown of gold and red, contains first a page of quotations on the art and importance of biography, then the letter, followed by an essay: "On biography and the significance of success." It is interesting to compare its sentiments with those expressed in *Literary Industries*, the Bancroft autobiography published two years later.

> Prospectus:
> To be a great benefactor of the race it is not necessary that a man should spend his life working directly for that end. He need not necessarily be what is commonly called a good man, or specially benevolent, or amiable, or charitable, or a person who professedly puts forth all his powers for the benefit of others.... Fortunately, in the economy of political and social affairs, things are so arranged that those results which are highest and best for the individual are highest and best for the community.[14]

> *Literary Industries*:
> It will not do for a man of affairs, if he would achieve any marked success, to allow any feelings of humanity, benevolence, or kindness of heart to stand in his way.... The most successful men in any direction, are not the best men. They may be best for civilization, but civilization is not the highest or holiest good, nor does it seem conducive to the greatest happiness.[15]

The language of the prospectus is gentler, and the role of civilization is viewed in a kindlier light, but Bancroft knew his tough customers too well to try to convince them that they had reached their eminence through altruism.

[13] [*Chronicles of the Kings, Prospectus*] (San Francisco: History Company, 1888 [?]), 1.
[14] Ibid., 5.
[15] Bancroft, *Literary Industries*, 785.

The brochure continues by arguing that if what a man accomplishes results in benefits to others, a record of his life is important to the community, his family, and himself, all of whom deserve to know that his work and his ideas have been set down permanently as he would have wished them to be. After a few pages of description and praise for biography in general, the direct promotion is resumed in the distinctive Bancroft rhetoric:

> In the absence of a crowned head with armies at his call, who and what are these that traverse mountains and seas to come hither on this conquest of nature, to subdue the wilderness, plant empires, build commonwealths, organize society, develop progressional institutions, and elevate and ennoble their race—who and what are these if not kings? It is eminently in every way fitting that they should receive the highest designation given as title to man.... Mr. Bancroft could not lay down his pen until this matchless work was done. With his own hand he must crown these kings.[16]

The prospectus concludes dulcetly: "The object herein is not to urge, but merely to offer an opportunity, with proper explanation, which it is hoped has been clearly done."[17]

In this campaign there was no reticence about the size of the work as the scheme of presentation of the biographies was designed to be part of the attraction to prospective subscribers. There were to be seven volumes, and each was to contain chapters on economic and social history among which the biographies would be set. The preface to volume I of the *Chronicles of the Builders of the Commonwealth*, in a rather unhappily conceived figure of speech, states that the men were to be "embalmed in the annals of their own time and country."[18] (The phrase was also used in promotional literature, and an unfriendly press was to make a joke of it.)

An extremely detailed chart was made, indicating by numbers just where each "king" was to be "embalmed," using occupations as horizontal coordinates and geographical locations as vertical ones.

16 [Chronicles, Prospectus] 11–12.
17Ibid., 13.
18 Hubert Howe Bancroft, *The Chronicles of the Builders of the Commonwealth: Historical Character Study* (San Francisco: History Company, 1891–1892), I, x.

The design, organizing some occupations by activity, others by area, is ingenious but rigid,[19] and the biographies, dependent on subscriptions, did not follow it in detail. They were not, as it happened, even able to follow Bancroft's modified design, as set forth in the preface to the first volume of the *Chronicles*.

This passage, probably written early in the campaign, states that subscribers were to be placed in the volumes according to the following categories:

v. I Sources of power and progress, and the influences early dominating America, particularly the Northwestern part thereof.

v. II Government—Officials, legislators, the judiciary, military, lawyers and political leaders.

v. III Agriculture—Agriculturists, irrigationists, orchardists, stock-raisers, and viniculturists.

v. IV Mines and manufacturers—Owners (of) mines, mining ditches, crushing mills, reduction works, and leaders in mining stock operations; owners of metal, wood, sugar, flour, fibre, electrical and chemical works; makers of machinery; fish and fruit packers.

v. V Routes and transportation—Railway, steamship, telegraph, telephone and express officials.

v. VI Commerce—Merchants, bankers, and insurance officials.

v. VII Society—Real estate owners, capitalists, educators, physicians, the clergy, men of science and literature, journalists, artists, architects, and actors.[20]

It is quite possible that the very neatness and preciseness of these plans were parts of the promotional design which Bancroft was not too concerned with preserving; they were not followed closely, and a later brochure indicated a plan to make the *Chronicles* a continuing work.[21]

Commissions for the biographies were not won by brochures alone. The "hard sell" of presenting the rate schedule and persuading the

[19] Chart cemented on back cover of [*Chronicles, Prospectus*]. Copy in Bancroft Library.

[20] Bancroft, *Chronicles*, I, x-xi.

[21] Single-sheet brochure in "Scrapbook of Materials about Hubert Howe Bancroft, his Works, and the Bancroft Library," beginning: "There is another feature of the Chronicles of the Kings...."

prospects was the responsibility of Stone's corps of salesmen. They called on the well-to-do after the prospectuses had been mailed and related a little anecdote concerning the poet Pindar, who, when a patron expostulated that he was charging as much for a verse as a sculptor would charge for a bronze statue, replied that the verse would outlast the statue and the people.[22] If the prospect saw no incongruity in the implied comparison of Bancroft and Pindar, the agent showed him the price list:

Portrait on steel as per exhibit D, with 4 pages print	$1,000
Portrait on steel as per exhibit E, with 6 pages print	$1,500
Portrait on steel as per exhibit E, with 8 pages print	$2,000
Portrait on steel as per exhibit E, with 10 pages print	$2,500
Portrait on steel as per exhibit F, with 12 to 15 pages print	$5,000
Portrait on steel as per exhibit F, with 25 to 30 pages print	$10,000

Promotional guides for salesmen emphasize an appeal to the "love of recognition and appreciation" of the prospects. Canvassers were to point out that: "For every man...a particular place has been reserved...and that place he made for himself, it being the very occupation or industry which made him what he is." But if the agents met with arrogance, they were to point out that the arrogant one's life would probably be written up anyhow, and wouldn't it be better to get it right? If the prospect thought the rates were too high, the cost of preparation and the exclusiveness of the company were to be stressed: "We are crowning only Kings."[23]

The first contract form simply bound the History Company to deliver fifty copies of the engraved portraits, closing with the statement: "I hereby request and authorize you to print and insert my said portrait in the *Chonicles of the Kings*, together with my Biography consisting of about... pages of print." A later contract form for *Chronicles of the Builders of the Commonwealth* was modified to bind the company to print both portrait and biography, possibly

[22] San Francisco *Examiner*, June 12, 1890, 3.
[23] Ibid.

after one of the clients, David Jacks, had refused to pay more of his contract than the deposit because the company was bound to furnish only the engravings.[24]

The contract having been signed, it was necessary to obtain the needed information for the biography. As this dictation was to be much more than the token effort requred of salesmen for the *Works*, canvassers were supplied with a set of fifty-six questions designed to direct their interviews. The canvasser might ask the questions himself or give them to the patron. The list begins:

1. Birth-place: nation, district, locality, or town. Physical environment, topography, geology, climate, scenery, possible effect of these material conditions on body and mind. General observations regarding their influence upon families continuously residing thereabouts, for generations, as to mental and bodily growth; differences or modifications caused or thought to be caused thereby.
2. Date of birth. The spirit and character of the times. Any events of general or local interest affecting the atmosphere into which the child was born: a period of disturbance or quiet, dullness or activity, progress or standstill.
3. The event of the birth; any circumstances or incidents directly connected with or relating thereto.

Question four explores the sociology of the community, and questions five through twenty are concerned with the family, its genealogy, the appearance and temperament of both parents and their influence on the child. The questions are as careful and detailed as the examples given. Infancy, childhood, and early schooling are treated in questions twenty-one to twenty-five, which are long, involved and repetitious. Twenty-four answers itself, and shows Bancroft's view of education:

24. What value does he place on this part of his education—learning from books—as compared with his subsequent education by experience, observation, association, friction and assimilation among men in the actual, practical affairs of life? What education seems to him now to be the most

[24] Ibid.

useful and best? In business or professional work which knowledge appears to him better, that which is *taught* or that which is *learned*?

There is no question which concerns higher education; most of the "kings" had none.

Question twenty-seven is very brief, as the subjects needed no prompting: "Circumstances of his coming west: what led to this change of base? How was he equipped: what his expectations? Incidents of the trip." The next question reached for material which would form the heart of the biography, accomplishment and character. It is detailed, but evocative and flexible, designed to help interviewer or autobiographer without confining him:

28. Business undertaken: beginnings and advancement in affairs; character of his enterprise; ups and downs; successes and failures; the entire story of his commercial experiences in the growth of the community, from which to obtain facts of general interest and to determine his factorship and individuality therein. This narrative should be given with the greatest completeness in order that the character studied may be viewed under the fullest light of history and his own acts. Specific interrogatories cannot be satisfactorily framed to bring out this information, in advance of the particular inquiry, but are readily suggested in the course of the investigation. But, under any circumstances, the subject of the biography can readily expedite and promote the study by, at least, outlining what has been his life work, speaking freely and frankly of what he has done and how he has done it. Let him take, as nearly as he can, such a view of himself as a disinterested neighbor would take, discuss motives, his methods, his plans, his achievements, his strength, his weakness, his sagacity, his faults of judgment, his conscience in traffic; did he ever suffer criticism—have his integrity assailed—how would he answer his critics.

Question twenty-nine is an encouragement to the biographee to "speak right out and right on, regardless of the form, order or style," so that the mirror might be held up to nature. From general considerations, the questionnaire moves to specifics. A solicitation of the subject's opinion on Chinese immigration is part of question thirty. Between the general questions on politics and religion are ten brief queries on current problems: the menace of communists and anarchists, the threat of European immigration, the wisdom of free trade as affecting the Pacific, the question of free silver, the virtues of prohibition, and the advisability of supporting women's suffrage to achieve prohibition. These questions, so out of character with the rest, seem to be asking support of the "kings" for some of Bancroft's pet concerns. Question forty-two, concerning the patron's membership in fraternal organizations, brings the focus back to the subject of the biography.

Subsequent questions touch on religion, perception, memory, comprehension, and moral nature. Parts of them appear merely foolish—what man would describe himself as "intemperate," or "selfish, exacting, harsh, sordid, unsympathetic?" However, these terms may have served as warnings of weak positions which needed justifying and strengthening. The final questions on the list concern marriage and children.[25]

The completed questionnaires were returned to the library where they were fashioned into biographical sketches. Although several manuscripts concerning political leaders are in Bancroft's handwriting, literary assistants wrote most of the *Chronicles*. Oak played no part in the biography, having resigned in 1887 because of ill health, but Nemos wrote the first five chapters of volume I before resigning in 1888.[26] Mrs. Victor wrote background materials on California railroads before leaving the library in 1889, having declined to do any of the biographies without an increase in wages.[27] Subsequently, Alfred Bates, David Sessions, Thomas Savage and other members of the library staff wrote many of the biographies.[28]

Bancroft, however, kept his usual sharp watch. In a letter directed to Alfred Bates concerning the latter's draft of a biography of Charles Crocker, the historian specified what was wanted:

[25] Copies of these questions in galley proof are in [History Company Records]. A typed copy is on the verso of David Sessions' manuscript biography of Alban Nelson Towne. Bancroft Library.

[26] Oak, "Autobiography....."; Gren, *Lychnos* (1950–1951), 50, 56.

[27] Victor to Deady, December 24, 1888, and July 9, 1889. Oregon Historical Society.

[28] Manuscripts for individual biographies written for the *Chronicles* are on file in Bancroft Library. Many are identified as "in the hand of" Bates, Savage, Sessions, or other assistants.

1888

Mr. Bates

Do not begin a life of Crocker by the mention of Stanford.

Write two or three pages of way up abstract preliminary [*sic*] leading up to the subject.

Moralize more all along

Character study

Get books from the library and make 25 to 50 pages more.[29]

In a later note to Bates, Bancroft expressed his dependence on the assistants:

Mr. Bates

In regard to your work on Biographies it stands simply in this way; I am pledged to give the biographies to the History Company promptly, as soon as they can be done after they are handed in. This is imperative. If you don't do it I shall have to get someone else. This I should dislike to do, as I know you & your work, and am in the main satisfied with it.

And so far as you are concerned, I am sure you will never find so good, pleasant, & permanent work again if you lose this.

HHB

This work will probably last for years, but it won't do at all whenever I leave town for you to stop work, for I shall be away a great deal of the time, and the work will *have* to go on.[30]

Although the brusque tone of this letter is in marked contrast with the friendly letters which Bancroft addressed to Nemos, the message indicates that the *Chronicles* were being turned out in the same manner and under the same pressure as the *Works*.

After the biographies were made up, they were returned to Bancroft and then to the subjects of the sketches for further editing. Many of the articles went through several drafts before the customer was satisfied—but satisfaction was guaranteed.

Bancroft was willing to alter a page or two of the *History* to increase the apparent majesty of the monarchs. The first issue of *Ore-*

[29] "Miscellaneous Notes for Crocker Biography," folder in: Charles Crocker, "Facts obtained . . ." [dictation and related materials . . . for H. H. Bancroft's Chronicles of the Builders of the Commonwealth.] Bancroft Library.

[30] Bancroft to Bates, [n.d.], [History Company Records].

gon II dismisses Judge Orson Pratt's conduct of the Whitman massacre case in the following words:

> It was pre-determined by the people that these Indians should die....
> There was not the slightest doubt that Pratt would go against the people
> in this matter. But he ruled as he did, not so much from any just or noble
> sentiment, as, first there was present no inducement to do otherwise...
> and secondly he well knew the country would be too hot to hold him
> should he do otherwise.[31]

This attitude may have reflected the sentiments of Judge Deady, arbiter of the Oregon volumes, as the two judges were not friends.[32] Pratt had also declined to give Bancroft material for the history,[33] and the historian must have been annoyed. The *Chronicles* won Pratt's interest, however, and he became a subscriber. Bancroft was moved to revise his earlier verdict in a later issue of *Oregon* II; the passage quoted above was deleted, and the following paragraph inserted in its place:

> The judge appreciated in all its seriousness, the responsibility of his
> position. He seemed to realize that upon his decision hung the lives of
> thousands of whites inhabiting the Willamete valley. He proved, however,
> equal to the emergency. His knowledge of law was not only thorough,
> but during his life he had become familiar with all the questions involving
> territorial boundaries and treaty stipulations. His charge to the jury was
> full, logical and concise.[34]

[31] Hubert Howe Bancroft, *History of Oregon* II (San Francisco: History Company, 1888), 97–98. There is no way of briefly distinguishing the issues, as both appeared in the same year.

[32] Matthew P. Deady, "Diary," June 21, 1884, "saw Harding and Bush in the afternoon. The latter invited me to dinner with Judge Pratt but I was engaged today at Holman's. Besides I thought if he wanted me at his house he ought to have invited me before I left home. For many reasons, I have made up my mind never to visit his house except upon a direct and pressing invitation and then it will depend on circumstances...." Oregon Historical Society.

[33] Pratt to Bancroft, February 4, 1880, in: Orville C. Pratt, "Dictation and Biographical Sketches." Bancroft Library. Pratt coolly declined to furnish Bancroft with reminiscences and recommended that the historian consult Judge Deady for particulars of Pratt's career.

[34] Bancroft, *Oregon* II, 98. (See n. 31 above.)

John Dewey Library
Johnson State College
Johnson, Vermont

The tribute is followed by a paragraph of general praise of Pratt's judicial ability.

A life of Leland Stanford was fully prepared for the *Chronicles* but was not included because of Stanford's refusal to continue his subscriptions to the *Works* (Chapter V, above). Bancroft revised a page of *California* VI to flatter Stanford as *Oregon* II was revised for Pratt. Because of Stanford's rejection of the *Works*, only Stanford's library copy shows the change. Where the trade copy contains the mere mention of his name as candidate for governor, Stanford's copy contains a cancelans leaf (pages 723–724) pasted to a broad stub. The substituted pages praise his statesmanship and promise in a footnote a full treatment of his life in the *Chronicles*.[35] Although the trade edition was published in 1888, and Stanford's break with Bancroft occurred the following year, this could have been, as John Walton Caughey implies, a statement intended for a subsequent printing which was deleted after the quarrel.[36]

Pratt's biography, however, was not only placed in the *Chronicles* but also published as a separate monograph, as were the biographies of several other subscribers in 1889.[37] These are hardbound with the name of the subject and Bancroft's signature in gold on the covers. The texts occasionally differ from the biographies published in the *Chronicles*, although the format is the same and each has an engraving of the subject as frontispiece. The slim volumes were published two years before the completed work and could well have been used by agents as samples.

Agents sold subscriptions readily. Commissions were sufficiently generous so that Colonel Hatch could request and receive advances of $250 each on his first four orders. His statement in one letter indicates that his full commission would be greater: "Please send me check for $250, and I will try to draw only a small percentage of my commissions until you can get portraits paid for."[38] This amount

[35] Copy examined Stanford University Library, March, 1969. Brought to my attention by Clark, *Papers of the Bibliographical Society of America*, XXVII, 12.

[36] Caughey, 297.

[37] Bancroft Library has copies of twelve different single biographies.

[38] Hatch to Stone, July 18, 1888, in: L. S. Hatch, "Letters to N. J. Stone." Bancroft Library.

would have given him a commission of only five percent on his $5,000 orders.

A vivid picture of a canvasser in action is given by the letters of Edwin W. Fowler, who worked the Los Angeles area diligently and reported his activities to the home office with engaging candor and high spirits. An early letter boasted of selling the first $5,000 order for *Chronicles of the Kings* to Daniel Freeman, a Los Angeles millionaire agriculturist, who not only subscribed liberally and purchased five sets of books, but offered his help to pay a subscription to put President Bovard of the University of Southern California in the *Chronicles* for $5,000 also. Fowler was touched: "Had it not been for his determination to put Bovard in," he wrote, "I would have taken him for ten thousand." The letter continues with a rather jocular complaint on the hardships of canvassing:

> This thing of dining with these blasted millionaires drinking champagne until you can feel it ooze out through the pores of your skin and then after luncheon to sit down and salivate a man for five or ten thousand dollars is no easy task.... You have to let these big fellows have their own way. You have to let them wine you and dine you and then you can get your hands in their pockets.[39]

Two months later Fowler was writing his employers from San Jose recommending a fifty-page treatment for another prospect William Squier Clark. "I believe Clark can be taken for $25,000 just as easily as he can be taken for five," he wrote to Nathan Stone. "I know you will think I'm a terrible man to hurry things up, but I do want to get this back before the old man dies."[40] In a separate letter, Bancroft was asked to give Clark special treatment. "I want to call your attention to the remark of Mr. Clark in the matter sent for his biography that he would not be made second to Leland Stanford or any other man in California," Fowler wrote, and then, pointing out Clark's desire to have his portrait first in some volume: "He says he won't have his portrait stuck back in the back part of a book where

[39] Fowler to Sessions, June 27, 1888, filed with: Hubert Howe Bancroft, "Biography of Daniel Freeman...." Bancroft Library.

[40] Fowler to Stone, August 13, 1888, filed with: William Squier Clark, "Recollections of a San Francisco Pioneer of '46." Bancroft Library.

people won't read it." The letter concludes by quoting a compliment from Mrs. Clark on the appropriateness of the title *Chronicles of the Kings.*[41]

Mr. Clark does not appear in the *Chronicles*; perhaps Bancroft was not willing to accede to his demands. Fowler's remarks in his letter to Bancroft about approval for the title *Chronicles of the Kings* seem to indicate that a change was under consideration as early as August 1888; by December 1889, as indicated in the facsimile of a contract,[42] the change to *Chronicles of the Builders of the Commonwealth* had been made.

The practice of taking an order for as much as the salesman could get at the time he presented the contract, and then coaxing the patron to subscribe more by writing a long biography to "do the subject justice" was a common one. Fowler requested this of Stone in the case of the biography of Governor Lionel A. Sheldon; David Sessions requested it of Bancroft in the case of Adolph G. Russ, and the same tactics were applied to Senator James G. Fair.[43] A sentence in the biography of Milton A. Wheaton seems to record the failure of one such campaign: "But to enumerate all Mr. Wheaton's forensic triumphs would occupy many times the space allotted to this biography."[44] Mr. Wheaton received ten pages for his $1,000.[45]

There are extended biographies in the *Chronicles* for which there apparently was no charge. There is no record of payment or other consideration from Lorenzo Sawyer, United States Circuit Judge for the Ninth Circuit (California, Oregon, and Nevada)[46] from 1870,

[41] Fowler to Bancroft, August 13, 1888, filed with: Clark, "Recollections. . . ." Fowler had better success with former Governor John G. Downey, despite the opposition of the governor's business manager. See: Julia Macleod, "John G. Downey as one of the Kings," *California Historical Society Quarterly*, XXXVI (December, 1957), 327–331.

[42] San Francisco *Examiner*, June 12, 1890, 3.

[43] Fowler to Stone, November 15, 1888, filed with: Lionel Allen Sheldon, "Biographical Material and Essay, Military Genius, 1888"; Sessions to Bancroft [n.d.] filed with: Hubert Howe Bancroft, "Life of Adolph Gustav Russ. . . ." Both in Bancroft Library. Information on Fair from San Francisco *Examiner*, June 14, 1890, 1.

[44] Bancroft, *Chronicles*, II, 283.

[45] Hambly, 1.

[46] In 1890, the ninth circuit was expanded to include Montana and Washington.

whose biography begins volume II. Two other judges, United States Supreme Court Justice Stephen J. Field and United States District Judge for Oregon, Matthew P. Deady,[47] were included out of gratitude for commendatory letters which they wrote for the *Chronicles*. The letters, of course, were sent to prospective subscribers. Daniel Ream received sixteen pages in volume VII, apparently for introducing five fellow townsmen to a literary assistant.[48]

Although Bancroft won subscribers for a little over one-tenth of the one thousand steel plates to which the prospectus had announced the work would be limited, the *Chronicles* was a financial success. One hundred and six people pledged from $500 to $10,000 (four pledges were for less than $1,000, six were for $10,000), and almost all made good on their pledges.[49] The History Company took in over $200,000 in subscription fees; the volumes were paid for by the subscriber separately.[50] The *Chronicles* did not, however, become "continuous and perpetual" as an early release had promised, because Bancroft's differences with a canvasser led to an exposure.

On June 12, 1890, the San Francisco *Examiner* carried on page 3 the report of a suit by W. C. Boyns to recover salary and commission due him as an agent for *Chronicles of the Builders of the Commonwealth*. The subscription nature of the publication was detailed, and the rates given, together with the Bancroft sales approach and the names of several subscribers with the amounts which they had paid. June 13 brought more details, and on June 14 the story was on page one of the *Examiner* under the head: "Fair's Footprints, They Were on the Sands of Time and Cost $5000 to Make." The story relates the difference in space and treatment accorded with the different fees, then treats Senator Fair's case in detail, alleging that Fair was induced to raise his original offer of $2,000 when the "literary agent" showed him the biography of John Stillwell Morgan, an oyster canner, which would appear next to his. In order to "go at the first of the great min-

[47] Field's letter was reprinted in the San Francisco *Examiner*, June 22, 1890; Deady's in the *Examiner*, June 12, 1890.

[48] San Francisco *Examiner*, June 13, 1890.

[49] Hambly, 1–2.

[50] Ibid., 2.

ing men of the world," and to "completely eclipse the promoter of the luscious transplanted oyster," the senator had raised his subscription to $5,000. The *Examiner*'s stories did not disclose that the publisher's father, Senator George Hearst, had paid $1,000 for a biography,[51] and Bancroft did not publish the sketch which was prepared.

Other newspapers and periodicals throughout the state featured the story. The Sacramento *Bee* thought that the law should take a hand in disciplining the Bancroft concern for the threat of blackmail implied in the "We-will-write-up-your-life-anyhow" approach to prospective clients.[52] The Los Angeles *Evening Express* professed amazement at seeing some of the "subjects" conducting themselves normally after "being caught in an act that should make the vainest woman blush, and which involved the gross dishonesty of imposture."[53] The *Wave* published a short satire, "The Rival Kingmakers," describing a confrontation of "Bankrupt" and Warwick in Hades, in which Bankrupt wins over the Duke, angry at the usurpation of his title of Kingmaker, by proposing that they secure photographs of Pluto and Proserpina for a "large work" to be called "Picturesque Hades."[54] The *Chronicles* had become a scandal and a joke.

Prospects of garnering more subscriptions seemed unlikely. The *Chronicles* as a continuing work was doomed. The best Bancroft could do was to collect his pledges, use what biographical material he had, and fill the books to a good impressive size with economic and social history written by the assistants.

The *Chronicles of the Builders of the Commonwealth* was published in 1891 and 1892. Volumes I through IV follow the plan of organization as set down in the preface to volume I, but V, VI, and VII depart from it to varying extents. Volume I, the "Sources of Power and Progress," gives a smattering of colorful biographies in all fields and geographical areas: William T. Coleman, president of

[51] Hambly, 2.

[52] Sacramento *Bee* (date unknown) quoted in the *Weekly Star* (San Francisco), June 28, 1890.

[53] Los Angeles *Evening Express*, June 21, 1890.

[54] *Wave* (San Francisco), June 21, 1890. All newspaper citations except for San Francisco *Examiner* in: "Scrapbook of Materials about Hubert Howe Bancroft, His Works, and the Bancroft Library." Bancroft Library.

the San Francisco Vigilante Committee of 1856, and Irving T. Scott, the Pacific Coast's first shipbuilder, appear among others, and the volume contains gratis biographies of Juárez, Junipero Serra, and four members of the Astor family (John Jacob I, William Backhouse, John Jacob II, and William Waldorf). It appears to have been designed to secure favorable reviews from papers and journals, which might well ignore the balance of the set.

The departures in volumes V through VII are probably caused by unexpected resistance from some prospective subscribers. Volume V contains a one hundred and ten page biography of Collis P. Huntington, one hundred and twenty pages on the Ames family of the Union Pacific, and biographical sketches of the Vanderbilt family. The Vanderbilts, like the Astors in volume I, seem to have been given space without pay. Both families were, at the time of publication, *the* leaders in New York society. Giving them space was likely to stimulate sales. Chapters on prerailway transportation and the telegraph complete the volume.

The textual material on railways has been moved from volume V to volume VI, where thirty-seven pages about Charles Crocker and forty-five pages about promoter George Sisson are "embalmed" in three hundred and nine pages of information about western railroading. In the remainder of volume VI, a scant seventy-two pages of general information on commerce is scattered among the biographies of eleven merchants and financiers. Men following the miscellaneous occupations which Bancroft had grouped under the heading of "Society," did not respond too well to his overtures, and volume VII contains biographies of several agriculturists for whom there was no space in volume III.

The biographies which accompany the dignified steel engravings in each volume are a little florid in tone for modern tastes. Individual notices often begin with a panegyric on a virtue which the subject of the notice is alleged to possess. Like the questionnaires from which they were constructed, they then move on to an account of ancestry, before detailing the early hardship and later success of the "builder." They are not without interest for students of history, as the independent publication of the biography of Leland Stanford[55] bears witness. The bias of self-praise tends to make them pompous, however, and the necessity for giving a dull man with $5,000 much more space than an interesting one with $1,000, as well as their uncritical approach, limits their usefulness to historians.

Bancroft's own feelings towards the *Chronicles* are difficult to determine. His biographer, John Walton Caughey, has pointed out that the pattern of poverty, enterprise coupled with luck, and eventual material prosperity probably appealed to Bancroft, who had followed the same path himself.[56] This intuition is seemingly borne out by the letter to Nemos, quoted earlier in this chapter. However, Nemos left no clue as to the circumstances of the letter, which may have been written in an attempt to persuade him to stay in Bancroft's employ and undertake the same duties with regard to the *Chronicles* as he had for the *History*. Nemos left the library for undisclosed reasons and remained on friendly terms with his former employer—but his pride in his work on the history suggests that he may have felt that the subsidized biographies of the *Chronicles* were unworthy of his efforts. Bancroft's later writings on the "Big Four" (Huntington, Stanford, Crocker, and Mark Hopkins—owners of the Central Pacific Railway)[57] are in flat contradiction to the *Chronicles* and hint that he, too, was not proud of the biography.

Publication of a sequel often reawakens interest in its predecessor. Because of the public outcry in the West attending the exposure of the commercial nature of the *Chronicles*, the biography merely cast further suspicion on the history and the Bancroft library. Although the faithful remained faithful, and favorable notices appeared in the San Francisco *Chronicle* and the *Argonaut*,[58] the common reaction was laughter directed principally against the victims of Bancroft's slick sales crew.

[55] Hubert Howe Bancroft, *History of the Life of Leland Stanford: a Character Study* (Oakland: Biobooks, 1952), 235 pp.

[56] Caughey, 315.

[57] Bancroft, *Retrospection*, 232 ff.

[58] San Francisco *Chronicle*, June 28, 1891; *Argonaut*, June 21, 1891.

The scandal did not reach the East, and the New York *Daily Tribune*[59] and other newspapers gave the first volume of the *Chronicles* excellent reviews. The New York *Sun* was certainly not aware of the subscription nature of the work when it published the following:

> The biographies of William T. Coleman and Stephen J. Field are carefully and sympathetically written, but as the subjects of them are still living, the propriety of including them in a work of this character is questionable.[60]

Unfortunately for Bancroft, the East was not an active market for either the *Works* or the *Chronicles*.

In the West, it became more and more difficult to convince the public of the merit of the *Works*, and sales continued to decline. The *Chronicles* had been a financial success, but their exposure made Bancroft vulnerable to attack from many quarters.

[59] New York *Daily Tribune*, July 6, 1891.
[60] New York *Sun*, August 30, 1891.

CHAPTER X

THE END OF THE CAMPAIGN

IN 1892, THE HISTORY COMPANY declared its last dividends, a total of $10,000 for the year, a very small amount in comparison with earlier years. In the six years since its founding, the company had paid about $300,000 in dividends.[1] Ten thousand orders had been taken in the ten years of the campaign, but the market had been oversaturated, and more than one-third of the orders could not be collected.[2] In 1890, both *Nevada, Colorado and Wyoming* and *Washington, Idaho and Montana* had been published in editions of six thousand copies, although ten thousand copies of *California* VII were issued.[3] Efforts to sell the *Works* as a set had been dropped by the most successful Bancroft salesmen in favor of the *Chronicles* campaign with its promise of higher commissions. The campaign for the history had been at a standstill since 1889.

Single volumes of the *Works*, however, enjoyed a brisk sale in

[1] *Stone v. Bancroft*, 23. Testimony of N. J. Stone. Stone gave a total of $285,000, but his figures for 1888, 1889, 1890, and 1892 add to $290,000, and he stated that dividends were paid in 1891.

[2] Ibid., 200–201. Testimony of H. H. Bancroft.

[3] American Historical Association, *Annual Report for the Year 1890* (Washington: Government Printing Office, 1891), 118.

[4] "Agent's Orders for Bancroft's Works, June 9, 1889–May 23, 1890." [Single sheets used for ordering individual volumes.] Bancroft Library.

1889 and 1890.[4] This sale could not fail to antagonize many subscribers who bought the set to secure a history of their own region. Canvassers had urged the set on patrons with the promise that it would never be fragmented. Their promise had been supported by the History Company, which had published a pamphlet entitled *Bancroft's Works—Why They Cannot Be Sold Except as a Complete, Unbroken Series.*[5] The selling of single copies appears to be a violation of agreement with the subscriber, although the agreement did not appear in subscribers' contracts. Such violations were all too common in the subscription trade, where books were frequently dumped on booksellers for sale at reduced rates after their subscription sale had subsided.

Custom was no comfort to frustrated subscribers, and many refused to continue to pay for unwanted books. The History Company filed several suits in Stockton, California, where its law department was located. Courts there refused to entertain suits against subscribers in other counties, and the California Supreme Court sustained the local courts' view of their jurisdiction.[6] If other suits were filed, they did not reach the Supreme Court, and there were too many defaulters to attempt action against all of them. In 1893 Bancroft estimated that about four thousand out of ten thousand orders were "bad."[7]

Bancroft attributed falling sales to Stone's mismanagement, and his dissatisfaction was nourished by a former canvasser, George H. Morrison, who was anxious to secure Stone's position as vice-president of the History Company for himself. In a letter addressed to Bancroft, Morrison protested his own fealty, alluded to the lack of interest of "others" in pushing History Company affairs, and indicated his willingness to serve: "If you should come to the conclusion that for any reason *you want* to *make* a change in officers, I would

[5] *Bancroft's Works—Why They Cannot Be Sold Except as a Complete, Unbroken Series* (San Francisco: History Company, [188]) [4]pp.

[6] *History Company v. Charles Light, as Justice of Peace of Stockton Township.* Supreme Court, State of California: nos. 15046 and 18001; *History Company v. Superior Court of County of San Joaquin.* Supreme Court, State of California: nos. 15120 and 15994. California State Archives.

[7] *Stone v. Bancroft*, 200. Testimony of H. H. Bancroft.

be glad to see Tom Dorland Secretary and Treasurer, and I would be glad to accept V. P. . . ."[8]

In 1892 the History Company was moribund. Sales had dropped drastically, and capital (which consisted primarily of unfilled orders) had been dissipated in dividends.[9] Stone continued to make collections but could produce no new flurries of sales. He and his employer were both nervous, energetic men; the tension between them grew as Morrison pressed closer to Bancroft.

In May it exploded. Stone accused Bancroft of conspiring with Morrison to put him out and threatened to sue.[10] Bancroft, after allegedly threatening to "begger" Stone and his family[11] (an accusation he denied),[12] put Morrison in Stone's place as vice-president and director of the History Company. Bancroft then sued his former vice-president for $107,000 in order to deprive him of his stock and break the ten-year contract under which Stone had worked since 1886.[13] Stone seethed with anger and frustration but continued to report for work even after his $350 a month salary was stopped on July 1, 1892.[14]

When Bancroft denied him his salary, Stone aired his grievances to a San Francisco *Chronicle* reporter, blaming the fact that he and his agents had been unable to sell twenty thousand sets of the history on the method of writing it. The use of assistants of various skills, he asserted, made the publication "nothing more than a compendium of the individual opinions of various writers who possess comparatively little merit." He alleged further that Bancroft had succeeded "in making the work utterly unsalable" by slighting references in various volumes to Protestants, Catholics, and Jews.[15]

---

[8] Ibid., 159–160. Letter, Morrison to Bancroft, February 13, 1892, introduced as plaintiff's exhibit.

[9] Ibid., 166. Testimony of H. H. Bancroft.

[10] Ibid., 23. Testimony of N. J. Stone.

[11] Ibid., 93–95. Testimony of Nyna Hambly. Also, ibid., 98. Testimony of Elinor Hayes, and ibid., 101. Testimony of F. C. Staib.

[12] Ibid., 169–171. Testimony of H. H. Bancroft.

[13] Ibid., 30. Testimony of N. J. Stone; also San Francisco *Bulletin*, May 19, 1892.

[14] *Stone v. Bancroft*, 6. Testimony of N. J. Stone.

[15] San Francisco *Chronicle*, July 9, 1892.

If the *Works* needed a coup de grace, Stone had given it. The History Company lingered on, party to suits, but publishing no more books. In September 1892 Bancroft filed articles of incorporation for the California Book Company, naming as directors Morrison, T. A. C. Dorland, Mrs. Morrison, and Mrs. Bancroft. The purpose of the corporation, according to the articles of incorporation, was: "The publishing of books or engaging in any other mercantile or manufacturing business."[16]

The purpose of the California Book Company seems actually to have been to put the assets of the History Company out of Stone's reach, as he was suing the History Company for breach of contract. When, on the advice of counsel, he dropped the suits against the History Company and sued Bancroft, the California Book Company disappeared. It had printed some letterheads, allegedly accepted a manuscript from José Trigo, a Mexican employee of Bancroft's, advertised a subscription publication, *The Book of the Fair*, but it had published nothing.[17]

Bancroft found Stone's presence in the History Building intolerable, but neither man would yield. Stone persisted in reporting for work in order to fulfill his contract; Bancroft had Stone's mail opened, his desk moved about, and at one time was reported to have shouted at him: "Shut up, or I'll throw you out the window!" He did not discharge him.[18] Stone, on his part, was said to have shaken his fist at his employer, and to have refused to talk to him.[19]

Although Stone, in the spring of 1893, became interested in promoting *Femina*, a book of medical advice for women, and devoted some time to it,[20] he continued to maintain his readiness to work for the History Company. In August Bancroft reversed his stand and made an offer to put Stone in charge of the History Company to

16 "Articles of Incorporation of the California Book Company," September 14, 1892. California State Archives.

17 [History Company Papers] (Sample of letterhead); also *Stone v. Bancroft*, 119–120. Testimony of José Trigo, and *Publishers' Weekly*, XLII (October 29, 1892), 696.

18 *Stone v. Bancroft*, 31–81, *passim*. Testimony of N. J. Stone.

19 Ibid., 169–171. Testimony of H. H. Bancroft.

20 Ibid., 36–57. Testimony of N. J. Stone.

work *The Book of the Fair* on the Pacific Coast,[21] an amazing offer under the circumstances which contradicts Bancroft's later allegation that Stone ruined the business. Bancroft, while commending Stone's ability, would not pay him for the months he had been denied work, and Stone did not accept the offer. On September 21, 1893, he sued his employer for $4,600 in unpaid salary.[22]

Bancroft lost the case, and his appeals were in vain. The struggle was long and bitter, lasting from 1893 to 1905, and the History Company perished quietly in the battle. After orders had been collected and dividends declared on the collections, all that remained were bad debts, unsold histories, and electrotype plates. It is not possible to fix the date when the History Company ceased to exist, but it ceased to publish in 1893. In September 1895 George H. Morrison, filing a petition of insolvency, listed among his personal property 1,495 shares of stock of the History Company. They were not considered as part of his assets, and no cash value was set on them.[23] However, the History Company continued to be listed in the San Francisco City Directory to 1897, when Charles O. Richards, husband of Bancroft's daughter, Kate, was listed as president.[24]

During Bancroft's struggles in court with Stone, two of his assistants made public their shares in the history. Henry Oak, realizing after reading *Literary Industries* that his efforts were likely to go unrecognized, notified Bancroft of his intentions to publish his own story of the literary workshop. His letter to his former employer gave Bancroft the opportunity to buy his silence for $20,000. Bancroft brusquely refused the offer and wrote that Oak might say what he pleased.[25]

An account of the publication of *"Literary Industries" in a New Light* has been given in Chapter III, above. Although Oak included

[21] Ibid., 42–43. Letter of H. H. Bancroft to T. A. C. Dorland, August 9, 1893, introduced as plaintiff's exhibit.

[22] Ibid., 8.

[23] San Francisco *Call*, September 6, 1895.

[24] *Crocker-Langley San Francisco Directory* 1897 (San Francisco: H. S. Crocker, c. 1897), 858.

[25] The incident is related by Caughey, 334–336. As Caughey states, Oak's remarks in the letter indicate that he wanted to speak out much more than he wanted money.

much material on Bancroft and his workshop, he aroused less immediate attention than Mrs. Victor, with her display of four Bancroft
volumes at the San Francisco Winter Fair of 1893, labeled as the
Works of Frances Fuller Victor.[26] Bancroft could make no response
to her gesture, and local distrust of the history grew.

Seeing Bancroft's position and reputation undermined by some of
his closest associates, Stone, Oak, Mrs. Victor, and W. B. Bancroft
(the last named having sued his uncle over the ownership of some
Bancroft Company Stock),[27] the Society of California Pioneers expressed the resentment which many of them had felt since Bancroft
had published his account of California during the Mexican War.
Their spokesman, Willard B. Farwell, had no more first-hand knowledge of the events than Bancroft or Oak, who had written the
offending passages. Farwell had arrived with the first shipload of
gold-seekers from New York,[28] two years after the Bear Flag revolt
and General John C. Frémont's activities. He had, however, taken
great interest in the Society of California Pioneers from its founding,
served as its president in 1863,[29] and delivered orations when corner-
stones were laid for the first and second headquarters buildings in
1861 and 1884.[30] In August 1893 he turned his rhetorical skills to the
composition of an indictment of Bancroft's *History of California*.

Farwell's resolutions to the Society charged that Bancroft had
libeled Frémont, the Bear Flaggers, Commodore Robert F. Stockton,
and Johann A. Sutter, and that the entire *History of California* was
unworthy of credence as authority. A later paragraph stated that the
Society should no longer permit Bancroft's association with it as an
honorary member.[31]

[26] Caughey, 266.

[27] *Bancroft v. Bancroft*, Transcript on Appeal, California State Supreme Court,
August 23, 1894, 3–5. California State Archives. The date of appeal follows the
Society of California Pioneers' action by one year, but the original suit was filed in
1893. Caughey, 337.

[28] W. F. Swasey, *The Early Days and Men of California* (Oakland: Pacific Press
Publishing Co., 1891), 288.

[29] Ibid., 290.

[30] Alcalde *(pseud.)*, "Willard B. Farwell," *Golden Era*, XXXV (January, 1886),
628.

[31] Society of California Pioneers. *Misrepresentations of Early California History
Corrected; Proceedings of the Society of California Pioneers in regard to Certain*

The resolutions were adopted a month later, and in October Dr. Washington Ayer moved to strike Bancroft's name from the list of honorary members. Bancroft was given an opportunity to appear before the Society but, characteristically, refused to do so. In February 1894 the Ayer resolution was adopted.[32]

Bancroft must have felt as much anger on his part as did the Pioneers, for accuracy was his chief claim to distinction. He had summed up his attitude in the preface to *Central America* I, published eleven years earlier: "We hear much of the philosophy of history, of the science and signification of history; but there is only one way to write anything, which is to tell the truth, plainly and concisely."[33] In a few instances, he had modified his opinions concerning events or persons in successive editions of the history, but the changes had not tampered with the facts. The Pioneers had chosen their moment well, however, and there was little Bancroft could do against this ultimate indignity.

San Francisco newspapers gave the story appropriate space, but only the *Bulletin* put the story on page 1, commenting condescendingly about the large numbers of "wigs and bald pates" present.[34] The *Examiner* and the *Chronicle* carried stories on back pages,[35] but none of the papers wrote editorials on the subject. The offending passages had been printed years before and critical opinion had been divided then, but the Pioneers' action excited no new appraisals. It was an eccentric action by a curiously self-important group and probably had little effect on the general public's regard for the history.

However irritated Bancroft may have been with the Pioneers and with his former associates, he had the ability to turn his back on the difficulties of the past and to plan another venture. His attention during the suits and exposés mentioned was taken up with a new sub-

---

Misrepresentations of Men and Events in Early California History Made in the Works of Hubert Howe Bancroft and Commonly Known as Bancroft's Histories (San Francisco, 1894), quoted in: Caughey, 342–343.

32 Caughey, 344–345.

33 Hubert Howe Bancroft, *Central America* I, *Works* VI (San Francisco: A. L. Bancroft, 1882), xi.

34 San Francisco *Bulletin*, February 6, 1894, 1.

35 San Francisco *Chronicle*, February 6, 1894, 12; San Francisco *Examiner*, February 6, 1894, 12.

scription publication, *The Book of the Fair*, which the Bancroft Company began to issue in parts in July 1893. Twenty-five parts were proposed, each of forty pages, to be sold at $1 per part.[36] The work was an account, with photoengravings on almost every page, of the Columbian Exposition in Chicago, one of the most spectacular and optimistic fairs ever held. The work would be dismissed as a "non-book" today, but it sold so well that the author published a "Fin de Siècle Edition" for those who liked display. The limited edition (950 copies) utilized the same plates—with the insertion of a few ornamental initials and tail-pieces, but margins were immense, as the volumes were one and one-third times the height of the regular edition.[37]

The Book of the Fair was composed and printed at the Blakely Printing Company in Chicago.[38] The choice of press naturally had the advantage of convenience, as it involved no long shipments of the photographic plates.

The use of a press not located in San Francisco may also have meant that Bancroft was planning as early as 1893 to remove his business activities from that city. In 1889 and 1891 he had felt forced to cut prices to the point of no profit on retail books.[39] Resentment of his tactics was fierce among fellow booksellers. In 1895 Bancroft closed his retail store in the History Building[40] and devoted his energies entirely to writing and publishing.

If he felt depressed or defeated by any of the changes of fortune he had been through during the early nineties, he gave little sign of it. *The Book of the Fair* was followed by *Achievements of Civilization; The Book of Wealth* published in ten volumes between 1896 and

[36] *Publishers' Weekly*, XLIV (July 15, 1893), 52.

[37] Hubert Howe Bancroft, *The Book of the Fair; an Historical and Descriptive Presentation of the World's Science and Industry, as Viewed Through the Columbian Exposition at Chicago in 1893. Designed to Set Forth the Display Made by the Congress of Nations, of Human Achievement in Material Form so as more Effectively to Illustrate the Progress of Mankind in all the Departments of Civilized Life* (Chicago and San Francisco: Bancroft, 1893–1894), 10 v.

[38] Ibid., verso title page.

[39] *Publishers' Weekly*, XXXVI (December 14, 1889), 931; ibid., XL (August 1, 1891), 240–241.

[40] Ibid., XLVIII (December 14, 1895), 1156.

1908.[41] The set appears to have been an elaborately mounted vanity biography like the *Chronicles*, though on a nationwide scale. An early brochure included the following passage in a description of the work:

> A most interesting and important feature of the work is a list of the men of wealth now living or who have lived during the nineteenth century, given in alphabetical order in the form of brief biographies at the end of every chapter or nationality to which they belong...it will be necessary to restrict admission to these pages to those who are worth a million of [*sic*] dollars or more.[42]

There were two editions, a "Fin de Siècle Edition" of 950 copies, and an "Author's Edition," limited to 250 copies, which contained the printed name of the owner and the author's signature.[43]

Like *The Book of the Fair*, *The Book of Wealth* is designed for display with many illustrations and portraits. The set of volumes begins with tangible relics of wealth and power of the Egyptian dynasties, while later volumes are devoted to the mines, factories, and houses of American millionaires. The photographs are clear, the incidental art work deplorable, and the format colossal. It was Bancroft's last subscription publication, and, from the number of biographies included, it must have been remunerative.

Bancroft continued to publish his own writings, often adaptations of earlier works. *A Popular History of the Mexican People*, a six hundred page abridgement of his six-volume *History of Mexico*, had

---

[41] *Achievements of Civilization: The Book of Wealth; Wealth in Relation to Material and Intellectual Progress and Achievement Being an Inquiry into the Nature and Distribution of the World's Resources and Riches and a History of the Origin and Influence of Property, Its Possession, Accumulation and Disposition in all Ages and among all Nations, as a Factor in Human Accomplishment, an Agency of Human Refinement and in the Evolution of Civilization from the Earliest to the Present Era* (New York: Bancroft, 1896–1908), 10 v.

[42] "Plan and Purpose of the Book of Wealth by Hubert Howe Bancroft," 4. (Leaflet, 4 pp.) in: "Scrapbook of Reviews of the Bancroft Publications." Bancroft Library.

[43] I have not discovered information on subscription rates. The work is listed in the *United States Catalog* with no price given. *Publishers' Weekly* does not give it. Bancroft Library has the editions mentioned in the text.

been published by the History Company in 1887 together with a translation, *La Historia de Méjico*.[44] The same country was the subject of a new work, *The Resources and Development of Mexico*, published by the Bancroft Company in 1893. The book was designed to promote the investment of foreign capital in Mexico by stressing opportunities in agriculture, stockraising, mining, and manufacturing. It was encouraged by President Díaz[45] and may have been his idea.

Most of Bancroft's writing after 1890, however, concerned the problems and opportunities of California, particularly of San Francisco, where he continued to make his home. *The New Pacific*, a saber-rattling celebration of the Spanish-American War and of American expansionism, was widely reviewed. It was included in the New York *Times* list of the one hundred best books of 1899,[46] and was issued in three successive revisions to 1915. Other pamphlets and volumes were more local, more personal, or both.[47] He continued writing and publishing until the year of his death, 1918, warning America against Japan, urging the development of San Francisco into a world center of trade, defending the Chinese, but expressing hostility to almost all other non-Anglo-Saxons.

He became a polemicist, but he looked forward rather than back, taking a lively interest in the reforms of the Lincoln-Roosevelt League. When he was asked in 1916 for his opinion of a group of Californians including Frémont, Bret Harte, and Thomas Starr King, proposed for the National Hall of Fame, he rejected all of them, many in characteristically vinegary language. After expressing his

[44] Hubert Howe Bancroft, *A Popular History of the Mexican People* (San Francisco: History Company, 1887), 632 pp.

Idem, *La Historia de Méjico* (San Francisco: History Company, 1887), 620 pp. Copy in collection of New York Public Library.

[45] Hubert Howe Bancroft, *Resources and Development of Mexico* (San Francisco: Bancroft, 1893), vi.

[46] New York *Times-Saturday Review*, December 9, 1899, p. 830.

[47] Including: *Some Cities and San Francisco and Resurgam* (New York: Bancroft, 1907), 70 pp.; *Retrospection* (New York: Bancroft, 1912), 562 pp.; *Modern Fallacies: an Added Chapter to "Retrospection"* (New York: Bancroft, 1915), 30 pp.; *Why a World Center of Industry at San Francisco Bay* (New York: Bancroft, 1916), 47 pp.; *In These Latter Days* (Chicago: Blackley-Oswald, 1917), 548 pp.; 2nd ed. rev. (1918).

regret that he could not, under the rules, nominate a living man, Hiram Johnson, he proposed one recently dead, Lieutenant-Governor John M. Eshleman, who had drawn up many of the humanitarian and progressive laws passed while the California legislature was dominated by the league during Johnson's term as governor.[48]

In his last years, when the seemingly interminable stream of volumes had at last dried, and the *Works* sat solidly on the bookshelves of western homes—tangible property and evidence of culture, rather than an ever-present reminder of debt—Bancroft had been honored for what he had done rather than derided for what he had not. His accomplishment as a collector was recognized in 1906 when the University of California purchased the Bancroft Library for $250,000. Although the collector contributed $100,000 of the purchase price, the contents had been appraised at twice the net cost to the University.[49] The *History of the Pacific States* won recognition as an indispensable work for students of western history. In the *Annual Report* of the American Historical Association for 1912, Katherine Coman, professor of history at Wellesley, called Bancroft "the Nestor of chroniclers of the Far West," and termed the history "a mine of information on which all subsequent historians must rely for suggestions as to the course of events and directions as to sources."[50] "Nestor" was an inappropriate sobriquet for a man who had finished his important work at fifty-eight years of age, but the appreciation of the history is altogether proper.

In 1918, after a brief illness, Bancroft died. His passing received prominent, respectful notice in the San Francisco *Examiner*, his old foe, as well as other papers.[51] Each paper mentions only the Bancroft

[48] Dickson, *Historical Society of Southern California Quarterly*, XXXV, 214–217.

[49] Reuben Gold Thwaites, *The Bancroft Library: A Report Submitted to the President and Regents of the University of California upon the Condition of the Bancroft Library* (Berkeley, 1905), 16.

[50] Katherine Coman, "Historical Research in the Far West," American Historical Association, *Annual Report, 1912* (Washington: Government Printing Office, 1913), 155.

[51] San Francisco *Examiner*, March 4, 1918, 1; San Francisco *Chronicle*, March 4, 1918, "General news" section, 1; San Francisco *Bulletin*, March 4, 1918, second section, 1.

Library and the *Works* in summing up his achievements. The same
limited tribute was given by the Pacific Coast Branch of the American Historical Association, which he had served as president in 1911.
At the annual meeting following his demise, this resolution was
passed:

> *Resolved*, That in the death of Hubert Howe Bancroft the Pacific Coast
> of America has lost one of its most useful and uniquely picturesque pio-
> neers. With enterprise unbounded and with audacious courage, he created
> the conditions which make possible the first scientific treatment of the
> history of one half of our continent. His labors also endow the States
> and peoples of the coast with a priceless heritage of historical treasures,
> now placed at the disposal of scholars by the University of California. It
> is not our function to pass judgment in detail, upon the histories produced
> under Mr. Bancroft's planning, management, and collaboration. But as
> heirs and beneficiaries in a special sense of the work which illustrates his
> enthusiastic devotion to a life ideal, it is fitting that this association should
> recognize the great debt which all workers in any portion of this field owe
> to Mr. Bancroft as a writer, as publisher, and as collector of the far-famed
> Bancroft Library.[52]

[52] "Proceedings of the Pacific Coast Branch," American Historical Association,
Annual Report, 1919 (Washington: Government Printing Office, 1923), 114.

CHAPTER XI

THE BANCROFT CONTRIBUTION

ANYONE WHO attempts to appraise the permanent value of the pro-
ducts of Bancroft's most active years, 1860–1890, must begin where
the tribute quoted at the close of the preceding chapter ends—with
the collection of books and manuscripts that formed the nucleus of
the present-day Bancroft Library. The merchant-collector at once
arrived at a philosophy destined to make his library significant in its
time—comprehensive acquisition. Selection, confining his collection
to the "best" authorities or rare, fine editions, would have made his
library more admired by the general public of his day but less valuable.

In Bancroft's own words, the library contained: "Heaps and heaps
of diamonds—and sawdust!"[1] Contemporaries were quick enough to
see the sawdust. Many newspapers were shocked at the valuation
Bancroft placed on his collection, and their comments made it more
difficult for him to sell it. After the library had been rejected by the
State of California and neglected by Congress, it was refused by the
Consolidated Library of New York, although the latter institution
might be excused at balking at Bancroft's price, which had risen
to $500,000.[2]

As early as 1886, a president of the University of California had

[1] Bancroft, *Literary Industries*, 218.
[2] *Publishers' Weekly*, XLIX (February 8, 1896), 306.

mentioned the desirability of securing the Bancroft collection for the University.[3] From 1898 to 1905, the University took an increasing interest in acquiring the library, but public opinion and price deterred them. Henry Morse Stephens, a professor of history and friend of University President Benjamin Ide Wheeler, secured an offer from Bancroft to donate $100,000 of his asking price if the University would buy at $250,000. Stephens presented the matter to the Regents, who, wanting reassurance before taking action, appointed Reuben Gold Thwaites, well-known historian, editor, and superintendent of the Wisconsin Historical Society, to evaluate the collection.[4]

Thwaites' report, published in 1905, expressed his initial apprehension of finding that Bancroft overestimated his library, and his "profound satisfaction" that it took "high rank among the general collections of Americana such as exist at Harvard University, the Boston Public Library, the Library of Congress, the New York State Library, and the Wisconsin Historical Library."[5] The evaluation of the several classes of material in the library was given, and may be summarized as follows:

Manuscripts	$ 80,000
Documents, voyages, maps	25,000
Newspapers and scrapbooks	50,000
Rare books	20,000
Ethnology, linguistics, cultural studies	20,000
Printed Californiana	50,000
Local material including Mexican	55,000
Total	$300,000[6]

Thwaites stressed, at the conclusion of his report, that Bancroft's price of $250,000, fixed in 1887, was a moderate one for 1905, as prices on Americana had, in some cases, doubled in the intervening period. Furthermore, Bancroft's offer of $100,000 made the collection a bargain.[7]

[3] Edwin S. Holden, *Biennial Report of the President of the University to the Governor, 1886*, 30–31, cited by Caughey, 352.

[4] Caughey, 355–360.   [5] Thwaites, 2.
[6] Ibid., 2–16.   [7] Ibid., 16–17.

The Regents read the Thwaites report, decided to purchase the library and arranged with Bancroft to pay the $150,000 balance in three annual installments. On November 25, 1905, Bancroft accepted the University's note and gave President Wheeler the keys to the Valencia Street building.[8]

The historian must have taken profound satisfaction in the high valuation set by Thwaites on the library's manuscript collection. These included the mission, presidio, and Mexican governmental records which Bancroft had journeyed through California and Mexico to discover and have copied, fur company records he had secured in the Pacific Northwest, and the personal histories which he and Cerutti had cajoled from Vallejo, Castro, and Alvarado. In this class also were the many dictations which he had taken from early settlers in the West. The manuscripts were the unique part of the Bancroft collection, one which could not have been gathered at any other time or place—and which only he had the vision and persistence to assemble.[9]

Under the direction of a succession of scholars in its field, Herbert E. Bolton, Herbert I. Priestley, and George P. Hammond, the Bancroft Library has continued to grow, with the publications of these directors playing an important part in increasing its renown. Suitably housed in the Doe Library annex after several moves about the Berkeley campus, it remains one of America's outstanding libraries.

A more detailed discussion of the Bancroft Library under the University is not a part of the field of this study, but a consideration of the growing utilization and appreciation of its original product is appropriate. That the *Works* was not admired by everyone in the West is apparent from criticisms from some of the press. Colleagues, also, could be unfriendly. Another amateur historiographer, Theodore H. Hittell, wrote and published a four-volume history of California between 1885 and 1897 without consulting Bancroft.[9] To a friend, Hittel wrote that Bancroft had "neither the knowledge or ability to

---

[8] Caughey, 363. Further details on the Bancroft Library under University administration will be found in Caughey, 390–407. There is no detailed history of the Bancroft Library after its acquisition by the University.

[9] Oak, *"Literary Industries" in a New Light*, 20–21.

write anything worth reading, nor had he the skill or liberality to select or pay men who might have been able to do so."[10]

Other writers were more realistic. After criticizing Hittell's work, Josiah Royce, philosopher and contributor of a volume on California to the *American Commonwealths* series, wrote a letter to Milicent Shinn, editor of the *Overland Monthly*. In it Royce extolled the merits of "Bancroft," explaining that in doing so he was recognizing the merits of Henry Oak, "by far the first living specialist in early California history." The letter continues:

> This "Bancroft" is above Hittell because he has more authoritative sources and has worked much harder. I am sorry to have to attribute any part of this excellence to H. H. B. himself. I said that I was sorry in my review, using all the irony that I dared under the circumstances, and in view of my right as a privately informed person. But I made it plain that Hittell seemed to me poorer, not than H. H. B., in person, but poorer than H. H. B.'s book, a very different thing, as the public already knows, and will know more and more clearly as time goes on.[11]

In subsequent years, the distinction between Bancroft and his work persisted. The *Works* has achieved increasing recognition as an indispensable reference. Its painstaking parade of sources and full footnotes have stimulated scholars to further studies, and the fault once charged against it, the lack of a unifying, scholarly viewpoint has made it more durable than many historical works of the period. McGraw-Hill recognized the history's continuing usefulness by republishing the *Works* in 1968.

Bancroft, himself, always has been regarded by some historians as an interloper. In 1893 James Schouler read a paper before the American Historical Association criticizing the sacrifice of thought and creativeness to feats of technique and organization in the Bancroft method.[12] In 1917, speaking before the same society, William A.

[10] Hittell to Charles Fernald, June 10, 1892, in: Theodore Hittell, "Correspondence and Papers." Bancroft Library.

[11] Royce to Shinn, July 16, 1886, in: Milicent Shinn, "Correspondence and Papers." Bancroft Library.

[12] James Schouler, "Historical Industries," American Historical Association, *Annual Report for the Year 1893* (Washington: Government Printing Office, 1894), 59–60.

Dunning quibbled: "[Bancroft's] chosen sphere far transcended the customary bounds of formal political institutions; but whether his method of working the field entitles him to a place in historiography is still a mooted question."[13]

The question has not been laid to rest. Bancroft has been charged with inspiring a group of later historians, each of whom has sought fame in his own time through methods similar to those used by the publisher of the *Works*. Through the use of assistants, whose services are usually acknowledged, each of these writers succeeds in "emulating a factory or mill in making [his] name as familiar as the labels on cans by the very number of books to which it is attached." This whole school is damned for merely gathering data and presenting it facilely without exercising the "high function of judgment."[14] Less critical writers have been content to retell the story of the literary workshop—contributing nothing new, but keeping the story before the public.[15]

This continuing probing and recapitulation would have annoyed and possibly puzzled Bancroft. He had an accumulation of material too large for one man to handle, and he dealt with it in a novel way. His methods were business-like, and could even claim to be scientific, a quality much admired in the 1880s.

The presentation of a five-volume ethnological introduction to the history of the West was a manifestation of a new spirit in American historiography. In the late nineteenth century the discoveries of biologists and the speculations of philosophers had infected historians with the desire to be scientific.[16] By the time that Bancroft began to organize his volumes, history was conceived of as consisting of the

---

13 William A. Dunning, "A Generation of American Historiography," American Historical Association, *Annual Report, 1917* (Washington, 1920), 349.

14 Oscar Cargill, "Historians or Industrialists? Reflections on Bancroft, Winsor, Rhodes, Channing, and Nevins," *University of Kansas City Review*, XVII (Autumn, 1950), 35, 46.

15 E.g., Sam Acheson, "Clio, Incorporated," *Southwest Review*, XIII (Winter, 1928); John Russell McCarthy, "Wholesale Historian," *American Heritage*, New series, I (Spring, 1950), 17–19; John H. Krenkel, "Bancroft's Assembly Line Histories," *American History Illustrated*, I (February, 1967), 44–49.

16 Dunning, 349.

investigations of all phases of the activities of any period, rather than a chronicle of political and military events and leading personalities.[17] Bancroft felt compelled to give an account of aboriginal life because the natives were part of the story of the "Pacific States." The Indians had interacted with conquistadores, padres, trappers, and settlers, and influenced the history of the exploration and settlement of the West—they had to be explained. Significantly, the producer of the *Native Races* sought approval of his work from biologists Charles Darwin and Thomas Huxley, anthropologist Edward Tylor, and scientist-philosopher Herbert Spencer, as well as the author of *Hiawatha*.[18]

Although he rejected as outside his province any attempts to draw scientific principles or theories, Bancroft indicted a political approach to history merely in terms of the activities of its prominent figures. In the preface to *Central America* I, Bancroft stated that he wanted to tell the truth about the masses of people who came from Europe and America to subdue the wilderness and build new empires, and alleged that it was "historical barbarism" to throw the masses into the background in favor of a discussion of their rulers, who were "the creatures not the creators of civilization."[19] A full statement of what, in Bancroft's view, the people of the West wanted in a history followed his dismissal of the rulers:

> We would rather see how nations originate, organize, and unfold; we would rather examine the structure and operations of religions, society refinements and tyrannies, class affinities and antagonisms, wealth economies, the evolutions of arts and industries, intellectual and moral as well as aesthetic culture, and all domestic phenomena with their homely joys and cares.[20]

Bancroft's choice of subjects for his own writings—conquistadores, argonauts, vigilantes and the like—makes the fustian quoted above seem insincere. The reader who takes it at face value may be

---

[17] Ibid., 351.
[18] Bancroft, *Literary Industries*, 355, 338.
[19] Bancroft, *Central America*, I, xii-xiii.
[20] Ibid., xiii.

disappointed in Bancroft's history, for to the latter, "see" and "examine" meant merely to collate written records and make them into a narrative. He stated that he believed "the work of the collector and that of the theorizer to be distinct,"[21] and he did not attempt to carry out the analyses which might be expected after his statement of purpose. He recognized the scientists' insistence on facts, but he declined to follow the scientific method beyond fact gathering into the formulation and testing of principles.

For several volumes of the history, the materials on the whole fabric of a society were scanty. When his records were silent concerning the masses, art, and industry, as in seventeenth-century Mexico, Bancroft could find nothing to write about *but* rulers, however petty. The common movements come vividly to the fore in the sections of the history which concern the American occupation of the western states, where Bancroft could obtain dictations from the participants. Whether the dictations were written into the *Works* by him or his assistants makes little difference in their relevance.

Perusal of documents was expected of historiographers in the 1880s, and Bancroft was one of the first historians to make systematic use of information from newspapers.[22] The personal search for information from witnesses also took time. Bancroft's employment of assistants was logical and defensible. If his method had involved thorough personal revision and interpretation, as he claimed in *Literary Industries*, it might have gained favor. Bancroft was deeply concerned about completing his work rapidly, however, and he became an impresario rather than a historian.

Bancroft's historical method required capital, enormous resources of information, and a thoroughly competent staff of writers who would be content with anonymity, or something very near it. The process also must have a method of rebuilding depleted capital in order to continue. The scheme of selling the set volume-by-volume by means of subscription contracts was the only way that the enter-

---

[21] Bancroft, *Native Races* I, xi.

[22] John Bach McMaster, whom Dunning mentions as having been the first historian to make extensive use of newspapers (Dunning, 349–350) began publishing his work in 1883.

prise could have been financed, but the constant need to gain subscribers took more and more of Bancroft's attention.

He took the plates of his first work to a well-known eastern publisher, and then canvassed New England in search of critical approbation. Later he collected favorable reviews and forwarded them to his agents, and, ultimately, on his journeys for information for the history, he showed a pronounced concern for publicity and willingness to devote time and energy to self-advertisement.

Some of Bancroft's devices to build sales are reminiscent of those used by Prescott. The older historian, like Bancroft, had had plates made for his books before offering them to a publisher, not so much to preserve the state of the text as to make it easy for the author to offer the work quickly to the firm presenting the best terms.[23] After his books were published in England, Prescott asked that reviews be sent to him and forwarded selections of these to his American publishers for use in advertisements. He also suggested the reuse of commendations on his early works when new ones were published. In the late 1840s Prescott suggested to his English and American publishers that his nine volumes of writing, including a slow-moving title, *Miscellanies*, be grouped together and sold as his *Works—Miscellanies* to form the first volume with a portrait-frontispiece of the author.[24]

Bancroft was certainly aware of editions of Prescott's *Works* when he went to New York with his *Native Races*. He may have known that Prescott had earned almost $36,000 from Harper and Brothers between 1843 and 1855.[25] He knew that his work would be compared to Prescott's, and his initial rebuff from the Harpers must have been a blow. Critical success became a matter of pride as well as an economic necessity.

He tried to transfer this pride to canvassers for his *Works* who, in the course of their basic training in general canvassing techniques, were told that they must believe "that Hubert Bancroft in producing a series of works relative to the Pacific States of North America is

---

[23] C. Harvey Gardiner, *Prescott and His Publishers* (Carbondale: Southern Illinois University Press, [c. 1959]), 20–21.
[24] Ibid., 190–192, 199–200.
[25] Ibid., 219.

doing for the people of those states a great and lasting benefit."[26] The agent was expected to inspire his customers with similar fire, so that they would feel like patrons of learning.

When his appeal to the pride of the public-spirited citizen met with indifferent success, Bancroft appealed to his customers' vanity. If they wished to appear in his great work, they might tell their stories to the agent, subscribe, and take their place in history.

To assist his canvassers in gaining subscribers, Bancroft put one of his best men to scissors-and-paste work for newspaper advertising. He arranged for delivery of the books by mail or express, to free agents from the time-consuming problems of making collections. In 1885 the author went on a personal appearance tour of the Southwest with a pair of agents to try to boost sales. Still disappointed, he tried to bring returns up to his expectations by issung a vanity biography as a sequel to the *Works*.

His moves in modifying the conventional patterns of subscription-selling show a genius for improvisation in response to stimuli, for quick thinking rather than deliberate planning—the same personal qualities which led to the development of the literary workshop. These qualities led him often into problems with the people who worked for him, as he could be quick to anger where reason would have better served the situation. His treatment of Mrs. Victor and Oak led them to expose the workshop; some unknown slight to an agent brought the story of the *Chronicles* before the public. Under control, his tremendous energy was his greatest asset; unleashed, it could alienate his closest associates.

When the sale of the *Works* diminished, he quarreled with Stone, the man whom he had placed in charge of the campaign. From their statements in and out of court, the sale of six thousand sets was a disappointment to both.

But the *Works* had not only made expenses, it had paid the History Company dividends. These would not have been declared until all costs including salaries of literary assistants and other employees, composing and printing expenses, canvassers' commissions, allow-

[26] [*Strictly Private*], 1.

ances for review copies, and advertising fees, had been computed and deducted from returns. Bancroft declared that the "business never made a dollar, and it is over $160,000 behind today,"[27] but he was speaking in terms of his $500,000 capital of contracts and promissory notes. This capital, with the exception of a large collection of electrotype plates, did not represent the investment of Bancroft or any other member of the company. It was liquidated in dividends as the returns came in, and, though the returns were less than anticipated, the dividends amounted to about $300,000.[28]

In putting forth his history, Bancroft had faced problems for which there were no direct precedents; the production of a work too vast for one man to accomplish, the introduction of a nonprofessional, unknown author, and the development of efficient techniques to maintain a market for an extraordinarily long and expensive series of books. He was successful in solving the first two problems and did well enough with the third to make a profit.

The Bancroft enterprise was too specialized, however, to originate or develop general publishing trends. It is true that installment purchase of subscription works gained favor in the last decade of the nineteenth century, but there is no evidence that Bancroft's experience had any influence on this, as San Francisco was a continent's length away from publishing centers. Bancroft did modify current canvassing techniques in many ways to meet his own needs, but it is impossible in the absence of a detailed history of subscription publishing to attribute any practices to his example.

It is possible and important to summarize the influence of Bancrofts' publishing activities on the *Works* themselves. First, the vigorous campaign assured the completion of the history and made it available to all scholars. Almost every western library has a set. However, conditions of the campaign tended to modify the content. There were four such aspects: the decision to issue thirty-nine eight-hundred-page volumes, the schedule of one volume every four months, the involvement in promotion of sales by the putative author, and certain concessions to prospective subscribers.

[27] *Stone v. Bancroft*, 166. Testimony of H. H. Bancroft.
[28] Ibid., 23. Testimony of N. J. Stone.

The last named consideration, although it appears formidable, is perhaps the least important. Oak complained of concessions made by Bancroft to the Catholic Church.[29] *Utah*, according to an anti-Mormon paper, poured "whitewash" over the members of the Church of Jesus Christ of Latter Day Saints.[30] Mrs. Victor was apalled when her idea of including all of the early immigrants to Oregon turned into a full-fledged effort to enter the name of every subscriber to the history in the *Works*.[31] All these concessions and more were made to secure subscribers to the set. They were minor, however, compared to unpopular positions Bancroft maintained on Frémont, Marcus Whitman, and others. Oak admitted the concessions of which he complained were an improvement;[32] *Utah* also presents material unfavorable to the Mormons; the subscriber biographies may be overlooked, as they are not woven into the history unless their importance merits it. The concessions mentioned may flaw the work, but they do not affect its reliability.

Unlike the *Works* of Prescott, Bancroft's history was fixed in format when only a few of the volumes, the *Native Races*, had been completed. The decision was based on material in the library and estimates as to the importance and relative interest of the content proposed for each volume. Inevitably there were a few miscalculations. Only Bancroft has complained of the necessity to condense, but there are passages in several volumes written simply to fill space. Two chapters of seemingly aimless ramblings begin *Literary Industries*; the Modoc War appears irrelevantly in *California Inter Pocula*; and *Essays and Miscellany* was padded to the required length of 750 pages by Nemos at Bancroft's request.[33] Nemos was also asked for advice on the manner in which *Central America* I and III should be concluded.[34]

Although the bulk requirement occasionally creates arid or over-

[29] Oak, *"Literary Industries" in a New Light*, 36.
[30] Salt Lake City *Tribune*, December 24, 1884.
[31] Victor to Deady, June 18, 1883, Oregon Historical Society.
[32] Oak, *"Literary Industries" in a New Light*, 36.
[33] Bancroft to Nemos, May 20, and May 24, 1888. Nos. 40b, 40a.
[34] Bancroft to Nemos, October 17, 1885 and undated. Nos. 26b, 28.

flowery passages in the *Works*, it did not have as much effect on content as the pace at which most of the volumes had to be written. There was little time for the assistants to do more than assimilate and record information in time to meet deadlines, and Bancroft was able only to look at the proofs of their work. Occasionally, discontented with what he saw, he would demand it be rewritten, more often the proof would be returned with minor corrections and interpolations. There was no time to synthesize. Even the planning of some of the volumes had to be left to Nemos and Oak. Oak realized that the product was not history in the classic sense and devoted several pages of his account of his work to defending the value of annals.[35]

Bancroft's early experience with Appleton when, like Prescott, he furnished his publisher with plates and prodded him with publicity had worked out less happily for the Californian than for his predecessor. The historian of the Pacific States was forced to devote his attention to selling his volumes as well as gathering more material to fill them. This left him little leisure for historiography as his letters to Nemos demonstrate. He professed to believe that the presentation of the truth was the limit of the historian's function, but his conviction may have been born of necessity. He philosophized freely in the early chapters of *Literary Industries*, cluttering his pages with borrowed aphorisms. Faced with mountains of proof, as he was most of the time, he restricted himself to corrections which would increase clarity. As he had no time to cogitate over the spadework of his assistants, to formulate and prove or discard theories, everything which was turned up had to be presented and annotated.

The result is an exhaustive compilation of facts from the best collection of sources of the time with a minimum of theory. With its copious notes, the *Works* is a source itself, and has furnished information for readable popular histories as well as data for theorists, but it lacks the unity expected in a historical work.

Paradoxically, it is more valuable to historians today than a finished history might be. Fashions in history change, but a comprehensive record survives to meet new ideas. Bancroft's *Works* is such a record —shaped in large part by the manner of its production, publication, and sale.

[35] Oak, *"Literary Industries" in a New Light*, 69–74.

John Dewey Library
Johnson State College
Johnson, Vermont

LITERATURE CITED

(All works cited in the text are included here with the exception of untitled articles and reviews in the *Atlantic*, the *Critic*, the *Dial*, the *Nation*, the *Overland Monthly*, the *Wasp*, *Publishers' Weekly*, and the San Francisco daily newspapers. Full citations to the critical journals and to the *Wasp* will be found in footnotes to Chapter VII. References to *Publishers' Weekly* and the San Francisco daily newspapers will be found in footnotes throughout the text.)

BOOKS

Bancroft, Hubert Howe. *Achievements of Civilization; The Book of Wealth.* New York: Bancroft, 1896–1908. 10 vols.

———. *The Book of the Fair.* Chicago and San Francisco: 1893–1894. 10 vols.

———. *The Chronicles of the Builders of the Commonwealth.* San Francisco: History Company, 1891–1892. 7 vols.

———. *The Native Races of the Pacific States.* New York: Appleton, 1874–1875. 5 vols.

———. *Retrospection; Political and Personal.* New York: Bancroft, 1912. 562 pp.

———. *Works.* San Francisco: A. L. Bancroft, History Company, 1882–1890. 39 vols.

The Bancroft Historical Library. [San Francisco, 1887(?)]. 38 pp.

Bancroft Library. *A Guide to the Manuscript Collections of the Bancroft Library.* Edited by Dale Morgan and George P. Hammond. Berkeley: University of California Press, 1963–   . Vol. 1.

The Book Agent: a Manual of Confidential Instructions.... San Francisco: A. L. Bancroft, n.d. 61 pp.

Caughey, John Walton. *Hubert Howe Bancroft; Historian of the West.* Berkeley and Los Angeles: University of California Press, 1946. 422 pp.

[Clappe, Louise Amelia Knapp Smith.] *The Shirley Letters from the California Mines, 1851–1852.* With an introduction and notes by Carl I. Wheat. New York: Knopf, 1961. 216 pp.

[*Chronicles of the Kings, Prospectus.*] San Francisco: History Company, [1888(?)] 18 pp.

Gardiner, C. Harvey. *Prescott and his Publishers.* Carbondale: Southern Illinois University Press, [c. 1959]. 342 pp.

Hill, Hamlin Lewis. *Mark Twain and Elisha Bliss.* Columbia: University of Missouri Press, 1964. 214 pp.

History of Nevada. Oakland, Calif.: Thompson and West, 1881. 680 pp.

McWilliams, Carey. *Ambrose Bierce, a Biography.* New York: Boni, [c. 1929]. 358 pp.

Oak, Henry Lebbeus. *"Literary Industries" in a New Light.* San Francisco: Bacon Printing Co., 1893. 72 pp.

————.*Oak, Oaks, Oakes. Family Register . . . with Sketch of the Life of Henry Lebbeus Oak.* Los Angeles: Out West Co., [1906(?)]. 90 pp.

Overton, Grant. *Portrait of a Publisher and the First Hundred Years of the House of Appleton 1825–1925.* New York: Appleton, 1925. 96 pp.

Parkman, Francis. *Letters. . . .* Edited and with an introduction by Wilbur R. Jacobs. Norman: University of Oklahoma Press, [c. 1960]. 2 vols.

Power, Bertha Knight. *William Henry Knight, California Pioneer.* Privately printed, 1932. 252 pp.

Prospectus of the Literary Works of Hubert Howe Bancroft. San Francisco: A. L. Bancroft, 1882. 1 vol.

The San Francisco Blue Book; Being the Fashionable Private Address Directory and Ladies' Visiting and Shopping Guide. . . . San Francisco: Bancroft, 1888. 254, lxviii [6] pp.

Squier, Ephraim George. *Nicaragua; Its People, Scenery, Monuments and the Proposed Interoceanic Canal.* New York: Appleton, 1856. 2 vols., illus.

————. *The Serpent Symbol.* New York: Putnam, 1851. 254 pp.

Stephens, John Lloyd. *Incidents of Travel in Central America, Chiapas, and Yucatan.* New York: Harper, 1841. 2 vols., illus.

————. *Incidents of Travel in Yucatan.* New York: Harpers, 1843. 2 vols., illus.

Swasey, W. F. *The Early Days and Men of California.* Oakland, Calif.: Pacific Press Publishing Co., 1891. 406 pp.

Thwaites, Reuben Gold. *The Bancroft Library. . . .* Berkeley, Calif.: 1905. 18 pp.

Articles

Alcalde [*pseud.*] "Willard B. Farwell," *Golden Era*, XXXV (January, 1886), 628.

Baker, Hugh Sanford Cheney. "A History of the Book Trade in California, 1849–1859," *California Historical Society Quarterly*, XXX (June–December, 1951), 97–115; 249–267; 353–367.

Cargill, Oscar. "Historians or Industrialists? Reflections on Bancroft, Winsor, Rhodes, Channing, and Nevins," *University of Kansas City Review*, XVII (Autumn, 1950), 34–46.

Clark, George T. "Leland Stanford and H. H. Bancroft's History; a Bibliographical Curiosity," *Papers of the Bibliographical Society of America*, XXVII (1933), 12–23.

Coman, Katherine. "Historical Research in the Far West," in: American Historical Association. *Annual Report*, 1912, 154–156.

"A Cosmopolitan Publishing House," *Paper World*, 12 (March, 1881), 1–6.

Dickson, Edward A. "Bancroft's Lost Letter," *Historical Society of Southern California Quarterly*, XXXV (September, 1953), 213–220.

Dunning, William A. "A Generation of American Historiography," in: American Historical Association. *Annual Report*, 1917, 347–354.

Ferril, W. C. "A Basis for Western Literature," *Commonwealth* (Denver, Colo.), I (1889), 73–87.

Gren, Erik. "Herbert [*sic*] Howe Bancroft and Wilhelm Roos (Alias William Nemos)," *Lychnos* (1950–1951), 47–58.

King, Clarence. "Bancroft's Native Races of the Pacific States," *Atlantic Monthly*, XXXV (February, 1875), 163–173.

Mills, Hazel Emery. "The Emergence of Frances Fuller Victor—Historian," *Oregon Historical Quarterly*, LXII (December, 1961), 309–336. [This article listed in Table of Contents under title: "Francis [*sic*] F. Victor in Ascent, Western Hagiology Recumbent," the title listed appears at the head of the article.]

Morris, William Alfred. "The Origin and Authorship of the Bancroft Pacific States Publications: a History of a History," *Oregon Historical Quarterly*, IV (December, 1903), 287–364.

Parkman, Francis. "The Native Races of the Pacific States," *North American Review*, CXX (January, 1875), 34–47.

"Proceedings of the Pacific Coast Branch," in: American Historical Association. *Annual Report*, 1919, 107–120.

Schouler, James. "Historical Industries," in: American Historical Association. *Annual Report for the Year* 1893, 57–66.

Shinn, Charles H. "Early Books, Magazines and Book Making," *Overland Monthly*, second series, XII (October, 1888), 337–352.

Wagner, Henry Raup. "Albert Little Bancroft; His Diaries, Account Books, Card String of Events and Other Papers," *California Historical Society Quarterly*, XXIX (June–December, 1950), 97–128, 217–227, 357–367.

LEGAL RECORDS

"Articles of Incorporation of the Bancroft Company," June 21, 1887. California State Archives.

"Articles of Incorporation of the California Book Company," September 14,

1892. California State Archives.

"Articles of Incorporation of the History Company," September 13, 1886. California State Archives.

Bancroft v. Bancroft. Petition for Rehearing to Supreme Court, State of California filed December 30, 1895. 11 pp. California State Archives.

Congressional Record, 52 Cong., 1st sess., vol. 23, pt. 6 (June 4–July 14, 1892).

History Company v. Charles Light, as Justice of Stockton Township. Supreme Court, State of California: Nos. 15046 and 18001. California State Archives.

History Company v. Superior Court of County of San Joaquin. Supreme Court, State of California: Nos. 15120 and 15994. California State Archives.

Phelps v. Cogswell. Transcript on Appeal. Superior Court, City and County of San Francisco. 1883. 105 pp.

Stone v. Bancroft. Transcript on Appeal. Superior Court, City and County of San Francisco. 1895. 261 pp.

U.S. Congress. House. Committee on Library. *Library of Hubert Howe Bancroft.* 52d. Cong., 1st sess., H. Rept. 1795.

COMPILATIONS

"Criticisms on H. H. Bancroft's Works. A Collection of Newspaper Clippings, 1878–1887." 725+ pp. (errors and duplications in paging). Bancroft Library.

"Notices and Reviews of the Library and of the 'Native Races of the Pacific States.'" 3 vols. Bancroft Library.

"Scrapbook of Materials about Hubert Howe Bancroft, His Works, and the Bancroft Library." 1 vol. Bancroft Library.

"Scrapbook of Reviews of the Bancroft Publications." 1 vol. Bancroft Library.

Victor, Frances Fuller, comp., "Scrapbook." Oregon Historical Society.

MANUSCRIPTS

Bagley, Clarence Booth. "Papers, 1862–1932." University of Washington Library.

Bancroft, Albert Little. "Statement. . . ." 1 p. Society of California Pioneers.

Bancroft, Hubert Howe. "Colorado Notes," 1884. 4 leaves. Bancroft Library.

———. "Notes on Mexico in 1883." 209 pp. Bancroft Library.

———. "Personal Observations during a Tour of the Line of Missions in Upper California," 1874. 213 pp. Bancroft Library.

Bancroft, Philip. "Politics, Farming and the Progressive Party in California," an interview conducted by Willa Klug Baum. Berkeley: University of

California General Library, Regional Cultural History Project, 1962. 508 leaves. Bancroft Library.

"Bancroft Library Cash Account, December 1884–December 1886." Bancroft Library.

"Colorado Dictations," 1884–1887. Bancroft Library.

Crocker, Charles. "Facts obtained . . . ." [dictation and related material assembled in preparing his biography for H. H. Bancroft's Chronicles of the Builders of the Commonwealth . . . 1865–1890]. Bancroft Library.

Deady, Matthew Paul. "Letters, dictations and related biographical material, 1874–1889." Bancroft Library.

———. "Papers." Oregon Historical Society.

Hambly, Harry Bishop. "List of Subscribers to *Chronicles of the Builders of the Commonwealth* Stating Amount Subscribed and Paid." 2 pp. with cover letter dated October 4, 1936. Bancroft Library.

[History Company Records] Uncataloged manuscripts, including personal material concerning Bancroft and correspondence prior to founding of History Company. Bancroft Library.

Hittel, Theodore, "Correspondence and Papers." Bancroft Library.

Nemos, William [*pseud.*] "Besvuren Angift af den förnämsta Skrifvars & Redaktn of Bancroft's History of the Pacific States." (Swedish and English) San Francisco, July 31, 1888. Microfilm copy of original in Königliches Bibliothek, Stockholm. Bancroft Library.

Oak, Henry Lebbeus. "Correspondence and Papers." Bancroft Library.

Pratt, Orville C. "Dictation and Biographical Sketches." Bancroft Library.

Savage, Thomas. "Report of Labor on Archives and Processing Material for History of California." 1 vol. Bancroft Library.

Shinn, Milicent. "Correspondence and Papers, ca. 1882–1906." Bancroft Library.

"Utah Dictations," 1885(?)–1888. Bancroft Library.

LETTERS

Bancroft, Hubert Howe to Benjamin I. Hayes, March 16, 1875. California State Library.

———. to Edward Huggins, July 9, 1878. Henry E. Huntington Library.

———. to William Nemos, 1883–1891. Microfilm copies of originals in Königliches Bibliothek, Stockholm. Bancroft Library.

———. to Francis Parkman, January 17 and September 25, 1875. Massachusetts Historical Society.

Fowler, Edwin W. to H. H. Bancroft, August 13, 1888. Filed with: William Squier Clark, "Recollections of a San Francisco Pioneer of '46." Bancroft Library.

———. to David R. Sessions, June 27, 1888. Filed with: Hubert Howe Bancroft. "Biography of Daniel Freeman." Bancroft Library.

———. to Nathan J. Stone, August 13, 1888. Filed with: William Squier Clark, "Recollections of a San Francisco Pioneer of '46." Bancroft Library.

———. ———. November 15, 1888. Filed with: Lionel Allen Sheldon. "Biographical Material and Essay, 'Military Genius,' 1888." Bancroft Library.

Hambly, H. B. to Charles B. Turrill, May 4, 1887. Society of California Pioneers Library.

Hatch, L. S. to Nathan J. Stone, "Letters ... 1888." Bancroft Library.

Sessions, David R. to H. H. Bancroft, [n.d.] Filed with: Bancroft, Hubert Howe. "Life of Adolph Gustav Russ."

Victor, Frances F. to Matthew P. Deady, June 18, 1883. Oregon Historical Society.

———. ———. November 3, 1886. Oregon Historical Society.

———. ———. July 9, 1889. Oregon Historical Society.

———. to Elwood Evans, January 7, 1880, in Evans, Correspondence and Papers, Western Americana Collection, Yale University Library.

INDEX

978.007 C548vc1   AAP-4735
Clark, Harry,   060101 000
A venture in history; the prod

0 0003 0211394 9
Johnson State College